Elizabeth Speller is also the author of *Granta City Guides: Rome* and a memoir *The Sunlight on the Garden: A Family in Love, War and Madness*. She lives in Gloucestershire, and is currently a Visiting Scholar at Lucy Cavendish College, Cambridge.

ATHENS

A New Guide

ELIZABETH SPELLER

Granta Books

London

Granta Publications, 2/3 Hanover Yard, Noel Road, London N1 8BE

First published in Great Britain by Granta Books 2004
This updated edition published by Granta Books 2006

A CIP catalogue record for this book
is available from the British Library.

1 3 5 7 9 10 8 6 4 2

ISBN-13: 978-1-86207-830-7
ISBN-10: 1-86207-830-0

Typeset by M Rules

Printed and bound in Italy by Legoprint

CONTENTS

INTRODUCTION   xiii
THE HOROLOGION OF ATHENS   xxiii
WHEN TO VISIT ATHENS   xxvii
PLACE NAMES   xxxi

The First Wind: South • *Notos*   1

The Second Wind: South-West • *Lips*   31

The Third Wind: West • *Zephyros*   53

The Fourth Wind: North-West • *Skiron*   71

The Fifth Wind: North • *Boreas*   91

The Sixth Wind: North-East • *Kaikias*   115

The Seventh Wind: East • *Apeliotes*   143

The Eighth Wind: South-East • *Euros*   163

RESTAURANTS, CAFÉS, SHOPPING AND HOTELS   181
FURTHER READING   187
INDEX   193
ATHENS METRO MAP   207

To my son, Nicholas.
Traveller.

In Salamis filled with the foaming
Of billows and murmur of bees,
Old Telamon stayed from his roaming
Long ago, on a throne of the seas;
Looking out on the hills olive-laden,
Enchanted, where first from the earth
The grey-gleaming fruit of the maiden
Athena had birth;
A soft grey crown for a city
Beloved, a city of Light.

Euripides, 480–406 BCE

Now seven-eighths of the *zebetiko* has become part
of my soul, the bouzouki rings inside me and stirs me
like a cry in the middle of the night, the eastern
voices seem inevitable, as if they had been part of me
all my life. The music is not music, it is speeches,
cavalcades of cars, emigrant workers, crowd-filled
squares. Now when I get up to dance – prompted by
an urge to bring on a certain sadness and
melancholy – what I see in front of me is not the men
on their knees clapping, not just the bouzouki
players' hands fluttering like wings. I see crowds, I
hear speeches, I see my father, dancing.

Nick Papandreou: *Dancing with my Father*

ACKNOWLEDGEMENTS

I should like to thank Tassos Anastassiades, Mary Beard, Nicholas and Miranda Bolter, Jo Brace, Michael Bywater, Tom Holland, Christopher Kelly, Daphne Koureatas, Petros Krystallakos, Katharine Reeve, Georgios Romeos, Abby Speller, Tassos Zenembissis and Sofka Zinovieff for suggestions, contributions, support and inspiration.

My thanks also to George Miller, best of editors, and to my indefatigable agent, Georgina Capel, at Capel Land.

And, of course, to Pausanias (120–180 CE), the father of all travel writers:

> ... In his description of the Senate House at Athens, mention of a picture there portraying the Athenians resisting an invasion of Gauls sends him off on a two-page history of the Gauls. A little further along, a casual reference to two kings of the Hellenistic period triggers a twelve-page survey of Hellenistic history. There are disquisitions on natural curiosities such as earthquakes, ocean tides, and the frozen vastness of the north; there are allusions to exotic birds and beasts – parrots, camels, the ostrich, the rhinoceros, India's huge serpents.
>
> Lionel Casson: *Travel in the Ancient World*

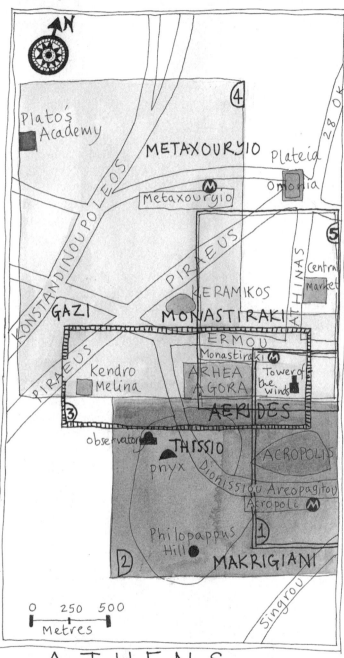

ATHENS ~

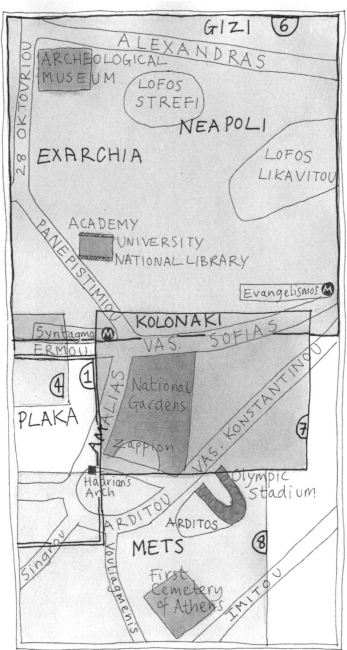

PLAN OF MAPS

INTRODUCTION

Four hundred years of Ottoman rule in Greece were violently overturned in the early nineteenth century and the independent Greek state was declared in 1829. At that time Athens was an insignificant town with just some ruins to her name. The decision to make her the new capital city envisaged an illustrious past as the means to a golden future. The Philhellenes, Romantics to a man – including Lord Byron, George Finlay and Sir Richard Church – who had volunteered to fight alongside Greek revolutionaries had certainly been motivated by a desire to liberate the ancient (and, they believed, common) heritage as much as (or more than) they had felt impelled to free an oppressed people. The German prince whom the allies placed on the throne of Greece in 1834 was the son of an ardent archaeologist monarch. Educated tourists had both an unquenchable appetite for ruins and large purses and in 1835 the Parthenon was the first archaeological site in the world to charge for entry.

From then on the revelation and preservation of antiquity was a priority. The Acropolis and the Agora were cleared of medieval and later housing to reveal the one asset that Greece possessed and that the rest of the Western world cherished. The reverence of later centuries for antiquity swept away much of the medieval, Byzantine and Turkish city.

The outcome has been that Athens is often thought of not so much as the sum of its parts but as consisting of only one part: the Parthenon. Remarkably few foreigners have any

The Parthenon

perception of the city beyond its two-and-a-half-thousand-year-old ruins and a problem with smog. These two images and the notions they represent have kept Athens high on the list of short-stay destinations for any traveller in pursuit of culture but low on the list for longer visits.

The glory that was ancient Athens ended in 529 CE. In that year the Roman Emperor Justinian ordered the closing of the schools of pagan philosophy that had been at the centre of Athenian intellectual life. In Athens, Christianity finally triumphed over paganism, whose temples were turned into churches and whose great buildings fell into desuetude and decay or were quarried for stone.

Other cultures and powers came and went but from the sixteenth century onwards, as interest in the distant past revived, Athens's ancient history became both its allure and its problem. There is a sense, even now, that Athens had no intermediate existence between an aesthetic and ideological high point in fifth-century BCE Periclean Athens and the frenetic modern city. The burden and beauty of a ruined civilization set up expectations that a modern city of 4.5 million inhabitants still struggles to meet.

Despite – or perhaps because of – having one of the most famous city landmarks in the world, Athens is unlike many other European cities in that its treasures and pleasures are not instantly accessible or on easy display. It has exceptional museums, theatres and other buildings but they need to be hunted down. It still has mysterious Byzantine churches, whitewashed cottages, pastel-coloured neoclassical mansions whose friezes, ironwork flora and fauna and elaborate roof tiles are slowly being restored to the grandeur they once possessed. It has *fin de siècle* arcades, art-deco offices and daring modern architecture – often conversions of industrial works to museums and galleries: **Technopolis** in the old gasworks to the west, **Athenäis**, once a silk factory, now a cultural centre, at Metaxourgeio, the **National Museum of Contemporary Art** in the old Fix Brewery at Mets, or the **Hellenic Cosmos** at Tavros. The modern **Megaron Concert Hall** on Vassilissis Sofias has fine acoustics and flexible space, while the new metro delivers education and art as well as reliable trains. Athens is also now a young city, an up-to-date European centre: a place of cafés, galleries, clubs, cinemas, and arcades of books, of fashion and gossip, Internet access, entrepreneurialism and fine food. Yet at the same time its eastern past, its Balkan present, create an exciting unfamiliarity.

One of the unchanged pleasures of Athens is that its culture, unlike that of many capital cities, is so distinctively its own. But it is also sometimes all too obvious that this is in no way a multicultural city. There are few ethnic communities: the proliferation of Indian, Chinese, Japanese and Italian restaurants that provides vast choice in London or New York is only beginning to make a mark here, although *fastfoodadika* has taken hold. Athenians are nervous, sometimes intolerant, faced with immigration from neighbouring countries in the Balkans, despite the fact that most Athenians are themselves descended from previous incomers. Yet the city will doubtless adapt again, as it has so many times, to absorb these changes.

Because for a city defined by its stones, Athens has always been shaped by its people. Athenian history and culture have been determined by successive waves of population: tyrants, armies, invaders and migrants from the Ancient Romans to the Turks to the soldiers of the Third Reich. Ottoman-influenced buildings were demolished or neglected when the Turks were removed, just as the post-independence flowering of nineteenth-century neoclassical architecture, seen at its most luminous in **Panepistimiou**, was eroded by the human dramas of the century that followed.

Between 1917 and 1923, the Russian Revolution, the post-war exchanges with Bulgaria and the expulsion of Greeks from Turkey forced 1.4 million refugees to enter Greece. Half a million settled in Athens and doubled the population. Hundreds of thousands of buildings were destroyed in Greece during the Second World War and the civil war that followed it. Islanders from the eastern Mediterranean Sea, desperate for work, came to a city of false promise.

This desperation, combined with financial opportunism, created a suburban sprawl of architecturally undistinguished apartment buildings to house the new population. The *antiparohi* system encouraged small landholders to surrender parcels of land not for capital but for ownership of one of the new flats. This inevitably favoured new building over restoration. Whole swathes of old houses bit the dust. From the mid-1950s huge schemes employed cement, unskilled techniques and speed: over 500 apartment blocks were erected in Athens in 1960 alone. The Junta of the 1970s instituted a further regime of destruction. More old houses crumbled, more apartments rose, and slowly the face of Athens changed. The infrastructure to support the expansion dwindled from affably muddled incompetence to impossibly and impedingly inadequate services, criticized at home and abroad.

Things came to a head when Greece was refused the 1996 Olympic Games. It had put in a determined and expensive bid for the centennial anniversary of the first modern Olympics – which had been held in Athens. The country, and especially the capital, was publicly humiliated as its infrastructure, its security,

Gazi

its pollution and its resources stood condemned by the outside world. The disappointment precipitated an heroic programme of restoration, culminating, rather to the surprise of outside commentators, in a very successful 2004 Olympics.

●

There haven't been any development projects of this magnitude since the time of Pericles.

Jacques Santer, 1997

●

For years, almost everything seemed to disappear behind hoardings: museums, roads, squares, monuments. But when they emerged again, the city was invigorated. Fine archaeological parks, beautifully landscaped, connected the great sites with each other. Thousands of trees were planted, and some of the most congested roads had been pedestrianized, turning them into leisurely boulevards. The recovery of Athens's neoclassical houses transformed many of its older streets. With energy, resolve and imagination Athens retrieved the heritage it still possessed: a fascinating, strangely seductive city that represents the history of a people, not just the ruins of antiquity.

. . . Although the Greek mentality is predisposed to indiscipline, chaos and obstinacy, the country has made extraordinary progress in the last fifteen years. There is an intrinsic dynamic that is forcing us to change. It is called competition.

Costas Mitropoulos, president of a management consultancy, quoted in *The Times*, May 2003

It is in the small things that Athens's character really emerges. For example, the little *periptero* – the kiosks on virtually every major street corner, invariably with a public telephone on the counter although mobile-ownership is one of the highest per capita in Europe and every old lady dressed in deepest black has a Nokia in her apron. The *Periptero* sells anything and everything at any time: Bic pens, maps, playing cards, cold drinks, tissues, nuts, aspirin, soft porn (the Athenians are more or less unbothered by pornography and *Playboy* sits tidily with any other glossy magazines on family coffee tables), newspapers and cigarettes.

Always cigarettes; it is still cool to smoke in Athens. At least half the population are smokers: ashtrays overflow, sexy

Periptero

women with eyes half-closed inhale deeply, shopkeepers gesticulate with sparks flying off their disintegrating Assos, waiters lurk in the shadows of their restaurants, having a quick draw, cigarette between finger and thumb, priests have a puff behind their churches, cooks stir their pans with a President always on the go. A staggering thirty-two billion cigarettes a year are smoked in Greece. The Greeks smoke more than any other nationality in Europe; they smoke in cinemas, in restaurants, in bed and at the dinner table (ceasing only to have long conversations on their mobiles). They smoke at the wheel of a taxi or driving a bus, or, more frighteningly, on their motorbikes. (They also wear crash helmets less than any other Europeans.)

Two and a half millennia after they invented democracy, Greeks are still vociferously political. Currently perplexed by the British, resentful yet faintly admiring of America, they are tense in their relationship with Turkey, despairing over the partition of Cyprus. They perceive sufficient external threat to continue to have compulsory military service, although many Greeks – not just the middle-aged – believe this to be character-forming, removing, as it does, young men from the pervasive gynocracy of the family.

Greek Independence is a matter of historic pride but there are those still living who remember the disastrous Great Idea, a period of Greek expansionism which ended in 1922 with the Asia Minor Catastrophe. They also recall the many times that democracy has been suspended, from the 1930s dictatorship of Metaxas onwards. The cruelties of the German occupation in the Second World War are unlikely ever to be forgotten, while the divisions of the bloody civil war (1944–9) that followed have never entirely healed. The oppressive regime of the Greek Junta, which seized power in an unexpected coup in 1967, was responsible for the deaths of many protesting students at the Polytechnic University of Athens on 17 November 1973 and only collapsed the following year. The banished ex-King Constantine, forbidden to return to his country, lives the life of an English gentleman in the leafy lanes of Surrey. The 17 November terrorist group, responsible for the murders of several foreigners and for long-winded tracts of Marxist polemic, has only recently been dismantled and is alleged to have been masterminded by an ex-student radical and opponent of the Junta now in his late fifties.

In times of peace and prosperity cities and individuals alike follow higher standards, because they are not forced into a situation where they have to do what they do not want to do. But war is a stern teacher; in depriving them of the power of easily satisfying their daily wants, it brings most people's minds down to the level of their actual circumstances.

So revolutions broke out in city after city . . . and in other places caused still new extravagances of revolutionary zeal, expressed by an elaboration in the methods of seizing power and by unheard-of atrocities in revenge.

Thucydides: *A History of the Peloponnesian War*, 3.82

Greeks will argue politics at the drop of a hat and are sceptical of all government. 'Oh, *him*', says a thirty-year-old Greek of an ex-foreign minister, '*he* was responsible for Greece's foreign policy'. His tone suggests that for a foreign minister to involve himself in foreign policy is akin to his taking an unreasonably large bribe. Athenians will shout, they will daub their views on a wall, they will protest for peace with Molotov cocktails. They are, despite (or more likely because of) this, passionately and endearingly pro-Europe. Few visitors to Greece speak the language, but almost all Greeks, however

Graffiti, Plaka

rudimentary their English, will make the effort, often insistently, to use it – or any other means – to communicate with foreigners. A Greek banker claims that every European country aspires to the values and style of its neighbour to the west and distances itself from its neighbour to the east. He may be right. Athenian Greeks are not mad on the north, either; they think Italy is the place – for Athens – to be. Italian fashion, Italian cooking, Italian films are all the rage. 'Andio' says the old man at Thissio station to a granddaughter gorgeous in skintight trousers and a cerise halter top. 'Ciao' she calls back as the train doors close and she heads off to freedoms her mother would have been ill-equipped even to dream of.

Athens is a city of many moods, ages and styles. Much of its charm derives from the varied layers and accretions of the centuries and the notoriously chaotic lack of a central city plan. It is a difficult city to know well; but perhaps because it takes time to fall in love with Athens, it repays the effort many times over. There are always surprises here: beauty, grandeur, tawdriness, mystery and entertainment – and through it all a tremendous energy and amused self-knowledge, which ultimately makes the city irresistible.

If you want the miles you travel to start earning for you, all you have to do is join the ICARUS Frequent Flyer Program!

This exciting new Olympic Airways program literally transforms your miles into privileges, since the farther you travel, the more benefits you earn.

From Olympic Airways frequent-flyer advertisement

THE HOROLOGION
OF ATHENS

The eight walks within this guide vary considerably in length and mood. Some cover quite long distances, others much shorter routes but in greater detail. Where some might be considered essential for any visitor to the city, others are decidedly self-indulgent. Together they reflect the unique blend of old and new, sublime and bizarre, serious and frivolous that distinguish a city in its prime. Some linger by a famous ruin, others in one or another of Athens's more unusual restaurants or *kafenion*, simply because so much of city life has, right from the start, been lived and discussed over food. However, for a visitor with just a weekend to spare, the major sights are covered in walks **1**, **5** and **6**.

The itineraries are arranged roughly along eight compass points, a scheme derived from one of Athens's lesser known but most charming ancient ruins. **The Tower of the Winds** (Walk 1), at the corner of the Roman Agora, is not the most famous monument in Athens; that honour lies, indisputably, with the Parthenon. But although two thousand years old, the Tower of the Winds is modern in a way that ruined temples, however splendid, can never be. It is actually a sophisticated Horologion (hour-teller) designed by the astronomer Andronicus Kyrrhestes in the first or second century BCE.

The Tower is an octagonal marble building. All eight sides once had sundials beneath the friezes, while two porches had fluted Corinthian columns and a pediment. It was originally topped by a bronze weathervane depicting a Triton. But what makes the tower particularly appealing now is the carvings of the eight personifications of the winds – winged figures draped and floating through the air, representing the different aspects of each point of the compass: Notos, the south wind, with a pitcher of showers; Lips, the south-west wind, steering a ship; Zephyros, the west wind, scattering flowers; Skiron, the north-west wind, with a brazier of charcoal; Boreas, the north wind, blowing on a conch shell; Kaikias, the north-east wind, with a shield of hailstones; Apeliotes, the east wind, carrying flowers and fruit, and Euros, the south-east wind, wrapped in his cloak. Under Apeliotes and Boreas are tiny holes to admit light and to the south are the remains of water channels that once ran from a spring on the Acropolis to operate the clock.

Ancient stone lion

The eight winds bestowed blessings and curses on Athens. Together their qualities contained the spirit of the city and shaped its destiny: showers and temperate winds for fertility; wet winters and dry summers for the harvest; breezes for voyages that built an empire and founded an economy; thunder and hurricanes for drama and the sense of supernatural power that underlies the Greek world-view.

When it was built the Horologion combined beauty, function and scientific endeavour. It was a sundial, a water-clock, a direction indicator, a weathervane and may also have been a planetarium. It made the real world and its possibilities comprehensible. It told the Athenians about their city and their place in it.

The busy streets around the Tower are still known as *Aerides*: the winds. I have used the eight compass points not as a specific geographical starting point for each exploration within Athens but as a broad indication of the area that each individual walk covers and as a starting point of the imagination for each walk in this guide. It became surprisingly and pleasurably obvious in compiling the walks that elements represented by each wind were still perceptible in the associated areas of the modern city.

Greater Athens is immense; information on a map is powerfully translated into breathtaking reality from the top of **Mount Lykavittos** where the city can be seen sprawled across the plain of Attica until it meets the sea and, year by year, spreading further up the foothills of the mountains. Yet the historic centre of the city is easily covered on foot, although difficult to divide up into discrete units. It is certainly misleading to think of Athens in terms of historical periods, leading downwards in worth from the Parthenon to the endless concrete apartment buildings of its poorer suburbs. It is a fragmented city, a mosaic of past and present, and that is its enormous appeal.

Different parts of Athens demand a different pace of exploration. Some areas, like Plaka, the Hill of the Muses or Monastiraki, are revealed best simply by immersion, wandering more or less at will, welcoming surprises and diversions; others – the museums of Vassilissis Sofias or the ancient sites of the Acropolis, for instance – obviously have very clear objectives at their heart. Whole books could be written, indeed have been, on the Parthenon, on Greek history, on archaeology and politics, so selecting the best or most interesting aspects of Athens inevitably leaves out almost as much as it includes, particularly those destinations that lie outside the central area these walks encompass. I have omitted detailed descriptions of the individual monuments of the Acropolis and the collections of the National Archaeological Museum. To do them justice would be impossible in the context of this book and there are excellent guides to both available on site.

Nothing else like the Tower of the Winds survives from the ancient world. Reflecting on its role, its history, its appearance and, above all, its spirit, this charming curiosity became an apt and convenient starting point for an exploration of Athens. It is not a museum piece. It is, like so much else in this city, a glorious survivor.

WHEN TO VISIT ATHENS

Athens is a very different city from season to season. Convention suggests that travellers should come to the city in spring or autumn to see it outside its predictable periods of incapacitating heat and the sometimes associated poor air quality of high summer but before the colder, wetter winter months. Yet preference for the spring and autumn really only assumes that Athens's ancient sites are the focus of a visit. In reality Athens's attractions are so diverse that every season has something to offer.

Athenian siesta

Spring is certainly ideal for temperature, although there are occasional rainy days. The city is fresh, the flowers are at their spectacular best, house martins nest all along the eaves. The less shaded archaeological sites can be enjoyed at leisure. Lent is exuberantly marked with carnivals and kite-flying and Easter is the great religious celebration of the Greek Orthodox church, with public ceremonies that are both moving and beautiful.

But summer has its charms. It is true that temperatures can occasionally soar up to 100 degrees from June onwards; however, they are more usually in the low eighties. In later summer the heat is often offset by a daily breeze. Athenians themselves say that July and August are frequently slightly cooler than June. Most hotels, restaurants and shops are air-conditioned and, in central Athens, covered arcades of shops and tree-lined squares have always made life, taken slowly, pleasant even on the hottest days. This is a time of silent afternoons while the city sleeps behind shutters or in park glades and then bursts into wonderful sociability late into the night. Athenians and visitors linger at cafés lining the streets, people-watching or, later, eating under the stars against a backdrop of dramatically illuminated ruins. The Acropolis is sometimes open at night in midsummer, there is *son et lumière* on the Pnyx and there are little open-air cinemas all over the city.

High summer also sees the exodus of large parts of the local population to the coast and the islands, especially at weekends. Some more traditional old restaurants shut, but they are few. Parking becomes easier, the city becomes quieter. The Athens Festival of Music brings outstanding international productions of opera, jazz concerts and ballet to the ancient Theatre of Herodes Atticus from late June until September. Its programme can be seen at www.greekfestival.gr and tickets can be bought next to the theatre itself or at the Festival Box Office at Stadiou 4 (in the arcade).

Neoclassical house, Plaka

The colours of autumn in Athens are stunning. The sky can be incredibly blue, the leaves of the trees turn, there are berries of every colour in the National Gardens, as well as autumn cyclamen. There is a sense of relief as the heat recedes and the streets of Plaka and around the famous sites become quieter.

In winter the city is certainly a very different but still handsome place. The more frenetic manifestations of the tourist industry die down. As the umbrellas retreat from the pavements, the interiors of the cafés come alive. Lights shine and conversation buzzes in *ouzeri* after *kafenion* after pastry shop, as Athenians continue to socialize and gossip. With its citizens wrapped in winter coats on the street or tucked in corner cafés playing chess or backgammon, Athens is in many ways more sophisticated from late autumn onwards.

Basement tavernas open, jazz and *rebetika* clubs come alive, the theatres and the opera company begin their winter seasons. During the last decade it has sometimes, though rarely, snowed in Athens. But it is relatively common, and a magical sight, to see snow on the peaks of the surrounding mountains – trips to ski on Mount Parnes are increasingly popular. There are many fine days when the whole city can be covered on foot and, above all, on the best winter days the light is simply unforgettable.

PLACE NAMES

All English writers about Greece have to confront the challenge of spelling. Rules for transliteration are still flexible; not only will different books or maps provide different approximations of Greek letters but even within Athens where English is used it is not necessarily done consistently. Fortunately, most street names – though not all – in central areas are displayed in both Greek and English.

I am indebted to Robin Barber's *Blue Guide to Athens* for pointing out one of the inevitable and delightful anomalies in this system. The street named after the famous Philhellene, Sir Richard Church, Odos τζωρζ – Church Street – has been reverse-transliterated back into English as George Street on helpful signs.

I have used the Greek convention of street name and number, e.g. Diakou 46.

THE FIRST WIND

South

Notos

*A youth tipping a
shower from his pitcher*

- The Monument of Lysiscrates
- The village of Anafiotika
- The streets, churches and tavernas of Plaka
- The Kanellopoulos Museum
- The Jewish Museum and the Frissiras Gallery of Modern Art
- The ruins of Hadrian's Library
- The Tower of the Winds
- The ruins of the Roman Agora

Pili Adrianou — Hadrian's Arch   Vivliothiki Adrianou — Hadrian's Library
Stiles Olimbiou Dios — Temple of Zeus   Megali Mitropoli — Cathedral
Romaiki Agora — Roman Agora   Mikri Mitropoli — Old Cathedral

Fair Greece! sad relic of departed worth!
Immortal, though no more! Though fallen, great!

George Noel Gordon, Lord Byron, (1788–1824)

Lord Byron is undoubtedly the most famous of British Hellenophiles. In Athens he largely escaped the notoriety that dogged his reputation in England and he remained a Romantic hero to the end.

Byron fought and wept and wrote for Greece. His vitriolic – though not contemporaneous – hostility to Lord Elgin's appropriation of the Parthenon marbles made him a champion among the Athenians and with many European aesthetes. His support of the War of Independence publicized and invigorated a cause, although Byron himself was to die of illness – exacerbated by rain, fever, bloodletting, doctors; nobody is sure – before actual battle at Missolonghi. His passion for an Athenian girl immortalized her in poetry. He loved Greece and Greece still loves him.

Byron's name is given to streets, hotels, indeed a whole district of the city, as well as to his statue and images; the beruffled, passionate poet, sometimes dressed in black, often in high romantic Greek dress, can be seen in settings ranging from museums to public squares to boxes of old cards on the flea market. On a plinth at the intersection of Vassilissis Amalias and Vassilissis Olgas, a half-draped matronly personification of Hellas crowns the caped and booted poet with a wreath. O Lordos Byron *is an Athenian hero:* megalos kai kalos, *great and good.*

Byron is associated with various parts of the city and its environs but it was in Plaka that he settled to write one of his greatest poetic works – Childe Harold's Pilgrimage *– in the*

Plateia Lysicrates. There, in a setting of mulberry and walnut trees, the graceful monument of Lysicrates stands in what must be one of Athens's most appealing small squares. It is the only monument of its kind that survives more or less intact. Built in 335 BCE, it celebrates Lysicrates' winning chorus in a festival of music and drama, and once the bronze tripod of victory would have stood on top. Subsequently it was believed that the elderly Diogenes lived and pondered here, while others claimed that it was where the orator Demosthenes resided.

Until 1826, when it burned down, a Capuchin monastery stood around it but the excavations of that ruin have been recently gravelled over and the monument now stands alone on a shady terrace beneath the trees. A small engraved stone simply recalls, in Greek, that O Byron *stayed here in 1810–11. Benches are set under the trees and the charming Diogenes café and restaurant – relaxed by day and chic by night, in both cases quite unlike its namesake – run along one side of the monument. It is still a fine and inspirational spot and remains quite recognizable from the nineteenth-century sketches of the area.*

The **Monument of Lysicrates** is a good starting point for wandering up and down Plaka. Dumped off cruise ships; en route from airport to islands; installed in language schools – the world eddies around the foot of Western civilization's most famous icon: the Parthenon. Plaka is understandably popular with tourists: a wonderful area of narrow streets, fading neoclassical houses, simple cottages and a tumbling mass of flowers – purple and pink bougainvillea, passion flowers and red geraniums, grown from earthenware *pithoi* or old olive-oil cans. It is a place of little squares deep in the shade of trees and the sudden ruins and names of antiquity. Above Plaka, always, the **Acropolis**. By day a grey citadel with the blue and white of the Greek flag limp against a sky as blue as the flag's stripes. By evening magnificent against the darkening violet light, every crevice and pillar thrown into relief by perfectly placed lighting, it is a stage set on which the Parthenon stands: a perpetual drama and a landmark which makes it impossible to become lost in the backstreets.

Plaka is Old Athens: the heart of the city. Indeed, for many who come to Athens it is all they ever get to see. Plaka knows its clientele – the graffiti is translated into English here – though the cultural gap is perhaps greater than the language one: 'Destroy the Philosophical Schools' is one of the more

Monument to Lord Byron

catchy slogans. Once Plaka *was* Athens; a town scarcely more than a village in size, clustered around its *acropolis*, on which several ordinary houses then stood. It was relatively late in its history, well into the nineteenth century, when the expansion began which eventually turned the city into the vast metropolis it is today.

Coming left out of the Akropolis metro the road leads across the pedestrian boulevard of **Dionissiou Areopagitou**. The rather imposing building visible behind the metro was once a military hospital for King Otto's Bavarian soldiers. It is intended that it will be the new Acropolis museum and study centre (at present exhibits are displayed on site) and this is where the Parthenon marbles will be displayed if they return to Greece. Unfortunately, the 1999 earthquake damaged the structure and it is currently closed. On the far side of Dionissiou Areopagitou is Vironos (Byron) which comes into Plateia Lysiscrates.

The shops around Lysiscrates make few concessions to tourism with their low corrugated roofs, dull green shutters, thick walls, and barrows of fruit. Behind these little businesses, fine mansions crumble away, currently picturesque, ultimately a disaster. There is an excellent wine shop at Lyssikratous 3: basic on the outside, its dark cellar-like interior nevertheless contains first-rate Greek vintages. The owner is a knowledgeable enthusiast although he is 'back in 10 minutes' for hours at a time.

The legendary *Daphne's* restaurant is at Lyssikratous 4; a town house whose vivid neoclassical interior glows with frescos in Pompeian red and where the best tables are in a courtyard set round a huge tree. *Daphne's* counts itself a superior establishment, and displays press clippings and photographs to prove it. The Clintons ate there, so everyone eats there. Service is friendly and highly professional, the rooms delightful, the glass and linen of the best. The menu is largely Greek with international spin: rabbit in Avgolemono sauce is one traditional dish cooked to untraditional perfection here. The wine waiter is happy to lure guests to rewarding Greek wines and steer them away from the safety of the familiar.

As the evening progresses, the social veneer cracks delightfully. By eleven, tables of strangers are blending, chairs are tipped back in cross-room conversations, photographs are being taken, a single diner is chatting to the musician. By midnight the restrained cosmopolitan strumming on a guitar in a corner is altering its tempo to the lurching syncopation of Greek folk music, and three men soon become seven, dancing, arms linked, with the tables pushed back. The waiters start to clap out the rhythms; the dancers, intense and sweating, complete the old steps.

Across the road from *Daphne's* a little *periptero* stands in front of the church of **Ag. Ekaterini**. In the evenings children play here, and on Sundays the priest can be glimpsed through a side window, omniscient in gold embroidery and heard all around the square. The sound of Sunday in Plaka is the chanting of the Greek Orthodox liturgy, relayed by strength of voice or, more often, by loudspeakers. It is a sound of the east. Bells ring, or rather jangle; there are no changes, no campanology here, no serious tolling, just a light and tinny call for attention that comes and goes from numerous small churches throughout the day. At the edge of the church's shady courtyard is a sunken Roman colonnade, possibly from a temple on a spot which may have been sacred long before Christianity.

●

I have taken up my lodgings in the Capuchin convent, belonging to the Propaganda of Rome. The choragic monument of Lysiscrates, which has been named the Lantern of Demosthenes, is attached to it and serves as a closet to the friar who has charge of the house. He has given me the use of it and I have no less a pleasure, at this moment, than writing in one of the oldest and most elegant buildings in Europe.

John Galt: *On Writing in Lysiscrates' Monument*, 1809–11

●

Following the upper, eastern edge of Plateia Lysiscrates a left-hand turn leads into Thespidos, a pretty stepped street, home to a colony of sable cats. What remains of the street climbs to the foot of the Acropolis. Turn right here and along the eastern base of the citadel and enjoy increasingly open views to the right across the city towards Likavittos. After a very short uphill walk along Stratonos there is a junction by a whitewashed church, **Ag. Georgios tou Vrachou** (St George of the Rock), which stands on an outcrop of the Acropolis. It is a little church of the islands, surrounded by flowers and quite different from the russet stone Byzantine churches of the metropolis. It is a clue to what lies ahead.

On taking the uppermost of the two lanes in front, more closely packed rural architecture appears. This is **Anafiotika**, a village within a city. In 1841, almost the entire population of Anafi, a barren Cycladic island, was brought to construct the new capital city. For their own houses they simply copied the white cubes of their island, exploiting an anomaly in the building regulations which said that if a house went up overnight, it was inviolable under the law.

Anafiotika

This second Anafi still survives and thrives, peaceful and improbable above the city. Simple single-storey houses clamber on top of each other up the slopes; all flat roofs, washing lines, chimneys, dovecotes and stacked firewood, with long flights of steps and alleys connecting one level with another. As tourists climb single file through the alleys they brush past men in vests sitting outside cottages on hard-backed chairs, while televisions flicker in inside rooms and cats sleep in pots of basil. It is not just the rough-rendered white houses or the cobbled lanes that seem so incongruous; the whole small area is silent, unhurried, caught between the hazy, noisy, modern city and the ancient ruins on the heights.

Every so often a rough-painted sign indicates the way to the Acropolis. One minute the path is tightly enclosed between abutting house walls, the next it emerges beside a little church to give wonderful views over the city and its ancient sites. This is the Byzantine church of **Metamorfosis tou Sotera** (Church of the Transfiguration of the Saviour), the highest point of Anafiotika. Immediately outside is the tomb of Odysseas Androutsos, a charismatic if slightly dubious hero of the Greek War of Independence, imprisoned on the Acropolis until his broken body was mysteriously found on the steps of the Temple of Athena Nike in June 1825. By the church there is a little stall selling cold drinks, postcards and snacks and a smiling woman sits opposite on a bench with her granddaughter and a large parrot.

The parrot, its white feathers tipped with citrine, is a jealous star. It preens, it forces its beak up to its owner's face, especially when she attempts to hold conversations with passers-by. It sees off large dogs but runs shrieking for protection when the perpetual cat disputes over prime sites on the Acropolis slopes get out of hand. Most of all, the parrot is a hoofer. It sings, not birdsong, but Greek songs. *Lah la-la* lah! it cries, *Lah la-la* LAH!, stamping its feet until its owner responds with the next phrase and it dances, very slowly, with its wings extended like an angelic Zorba, up and down the woman's arm.

●

> Very tall . . . sunburned face and breast, rude attire, immense bushy moustache, and bent brow.
>
> William Humphreys on Odysseas Androutsos,
> quoted by David Brewer

●

A few yards further on, to the right is the handsome cream and terracotta neoclassical house that accommodates the **Kanellopoulos Museum**. This is one of those delightfully eclectic museums which Greece seems to specialize in. Here are rich, dark icons (the best are the miniatures), the affable squid designs of Minoan pots, exceptional Roman sculpture and a hoard of medieval silver and paintings which has invariably delighted the acquisitive. It is perhaps at its best in the collection of personal possessions which make history suddenly real: alabaster ointment-pots, toys and jewellery from the magnificent – gem-studded weapons and rolled-gold bracelets with snarling beasts – to the very ordinary and very human: hairpins, beads, or seals. The museum is frequently empty and wonderfully peaceful (08.30–15.00, closed on Mondays).

From just beyond the Kanellopoulos, the view is marvellous. There are several options from this point. It is possible to continue along this path and reach the entrance to the Acropolis itself, or descend straight down to the **Roman Agora** and the **Tower of the Winds** via Panos. It is also almost irresistible to follow the winding paths in a north-westerly direction through the ruins of the old agora to the **Hephaeston** which sits on its knoll across the heart of ancient Athens (Walk 3). In the evening there are few better places to watch the sunset than here. The temple of the old blacksmith Hephaestus seems, appropriately, to be framed in fire as the sun goes down behind the distant mountains.

But to explore Plaka further, retrace the path a little and explore the network of streets under Anafiotika, taking any of the steeply descending lanes off to the right. At Tholou 5 was the **First University of Athens**, established in 1830 in an existing home. One of the first acts of the newly independent Greek state was to turn this private mansion into a university and it now has a

Street corner, Plaka

small but good collection from its own past – the medical exhibits are, as always, the most horribly compelling.

The spirit of Plaka is best experienced by simply exploring at will. This chapter will not suggest a specific route but will take one little-known street as being typical of many, and two roads at the centre of the tourist mêlée, and suggest that there may be more to them than at first assaults the eye and ear. It is hard to get lost here; all the lanes and steep terraces eventually fall back to Adrianou or climb to the Acropolis.

Plaka is quartered by two streets which intersect at its centre, **Kidathineon** and **Adrianou**, and its tourist hub is the **Plateia Filomoussou Etairias**. In these streets, more or less pedestrianized – the concept is a challenge to the Athenian love of the car – the flow of humanity from late morning to late evening in the summer is incessant. It is an area dominated by tavernas, cafés, restaurants, souvenir shops, jewellery galleries and carpet emporia. Shopkeepers and waiters importune, though usually with a smile and a certain lack of conviction; bands of very small gypsy children beg for money, the neighbourhood cats are plumper and sleeker than in most cities in Europe. They know all the tricks. Restaurant owners extol the virtue of breezy roofs preternaturally ten degrees cooler than the pavement. The street children – acting to a disturbing script – lower their eyes or take hold of your arm while trying to sell you their weary flowers. The cats are all hopeful affection interspersed with vicious assault.

Yet Plaka is very much more than this and its busy centre extends very little into the surrounding streets. At its hub,

Plaka view

identical plates of *souvlaki* or *moussaka* or Greek salad are served at one of a hundred similar, perfectly pleasant tables. Whether Athenian ideas of English breakfast or British ideas of Greek food are more misplaced is hard to judge, though there are plenty of opportunities to find out on Kidathineon and Adrianou.

In Plaka more than anywhere else close observation uncovers some real delights. An untidy building site under an indigo blaze of morning glory reveals the monolithic ruins of some ancient public building – almost any demolition in Plaka exposes the older Athens underneath. Above shops selling mugs in the ubiquitous Olympic orange and blue or postcards depicting winsome peasants – or ancient buggery in red and black – there are upper storeys with fine balconies, busts in niches and grand, shuttered windows while a shabby café down an alley may guard a perfect pre-war interior.

Tripodon is a street that may be on the point of losing its haphazard charm to official rediscovery. See it soon. In antiquity this was a noble thoroughfare, The Street of the Tripods, running from Lissikratous right round the base of the Acropolis to the **Theatre of Dionysos** (*Theatro Dionissou*). Its name refers to Choregic Monuments: the bronze tripods awarded to the successful sponsors of competitions in singing or drama and displayed on plinths to each side of the road. The Monument of Lysiscrates is the only exposed survivor, but bases *in situ* are still discovered from time to time, often in the basements of houses.

After leaving Lyssikratous and crossing Thespidos, the slight curve of Tripodon becomes one of the finest streets of the district. On the corner, a butcher's shop of the old-fashioned kind has carcasses slung on hooks while a large cage of yellow and sky-blue linnets – treasured pets, not gourmet food – are carefully moved throughout the day from one side of the road to another to protect their inhabitants from the direct sunlight. At Tripodon 30, **Figoures and Koukles** is one of the very last shadow theatres, an ancient eastern tradition which took on its own spirit in Greece. The nearest thing in Britain is Punch and Judy. Stock puppet figures – the anti-hero Karagiosis, the pasha's daughter, the tyrant, the policeman, the faded aristocrat and the good country fellow – fight old and new battles where anarchy rules, twice a day on Sundays.

Slowly the street becomes more elegant – houses of

different ages and roof levels include some carefully restored older mansions with ironwork balconies, careful potted roses and geraniums and wide double doors occasionally revealing the serenity of interior courtyards. Most of these houses stand on ancient foundations. At number 28 an appealing rose-pink and dove-grey neoclassical house contains one of Greece's leading heritage societies. They are always welcoming, speak English and can provide information on historic and environmental projects. They have a few items for sale: beautiful books on wildlife, history and photography, fine shawls, dried oak-leaf garlands, a handful of ceramics and jars of preserves. They also do simple organic lunches. But the house is really worth entering briefly just to see the massive section of ancient retaining wall from the Acropolis and a base of a choregic monument – both a contrast to the elegant lines of the later building and a potent hint of what lies underneath the whole of this district.

At Tripodon 14 is one of Plaka's nicest – no other word will do – tavernas. It has been there since 1935. The dark and beautiful gypsy children who descend on *Kouklis* clutching their mouth organs get water, a hug or a chat before they are gently led back onto the street and pushed in the direction of the next taverna. In a small house on two floors, full of family memorabilia, *Kouklis* serves *mezhedes*, brought to the table and selected from a tray. Flaming sausages – more daunting spectacle than delicacy – are the house speciality, but chunks of oil-dressed aubergine and baked octopus are tastes of the islands. Lunch on the veranda, under the vines, or (a particular treat) on a balcony made for two, could be served in any out-of-the-way Greek provincial town.

What looks like untidy rubble opposite *Kouklis* is actually an important ancient site. Some scholars argue for these being the remnants of the very first Athenian *agora*. To the left here, behind a car-parking space and on higher ground, is the

Taverna tou Psarra

twelfth-century **Ag. Nikolaou Rangavas** and, as Tripodon drops away slightly downhill, by taking a leftwards turn up a steep lane you come out by the tiny and delightful **Ag. Ioanis Theologos**. It is unspoiled by clumsy restoration and can possibly be dated back to the tenth century. It and the crooked little space in front of it – almost too small and certainly too irregular to be called a square – are among the gems of the area and there is an excellent restaurant, *Tou Psarra*, facing the church. *Tou Psarra* ('The Fisherman') specializes, as you would expect, in fish; but its chickpea purée, *gigantes* (spicy butter beans) and *horta* (basically field greens with lemon juice) offer rarer flavours and textures. The red-checked tables are set, sometimes unsteadily, under the plane trees, on shallow steps that lead up the Acropolis hill. It is one of the many restaurants that endorse their own supremacy with a list of celebrity visitors. *Tou Psarra's* claims are not modest:

'All Politicians and Vivien Lee (*sic*), Richard Burton and Larry Olivier' have eaten there. Presumably not recently. Even longer ago and less persuasively, this was allegedly the location of the Venetian cannon emplacement which, more by luck than design, caused catastrophic damage to the Ottoman-occupied Parthenon in 1687.

⬤

> With a fortunate shot on a powder-store, an inextinguishable fire spread this way and that, demolishing the houses through two whole days, and causing the enemy considerable damage and grievous affliction. Thus the greatly famed and celebrated fortress of Athens has fallen under the sway of Your Serenity's venerable domination.
>
> Captain-General Morosoni, dispatch to the Venetian Senate (from *The Parthenon*, Bruno, V.J.)

⬤

From Tripodon, streets fan out in every direction. A taverna at the top of a vertical climb is called *Sisyphus*, a vegetarian restaurant called *Eden* (despite everything they never ate the snake), and the students over-subscribed juggling and unicycle school – *Lazy Dayz* – stagger unsteadily out onto the street corner between Kiristou and Erehthiou. Narrow and plunging alleys reveal long rectangles of the city: a modern Athens of dense grey squares, tall offices and satellite dishes framed between old tiled roofs.

What are now picturesque lanes in Upper Plaka were once an area of extreme poverty. Descending towards Adrianou, the buildings reflect the much greater affluence of Athenian nineteenth-century expansion. There are some fine houses here, many well camouflaged by tourist accretions. The goods for sale, which supposedly represent Greece to those who want to take a part of her home, are strange mutations of her past and present culture: giant evil eyes, felt pompom slippers, fezzes, cheesecloth shorts and Gladstone bags. In Kidathineon and Adrianou a glorious regiment of bronze plastic helmets, brave with crests of red and aqua, black, chrome yellow and grass green turn shops into surreal military outfitters. There are swords too, of course, some substantial enough to alarm any airport.

Kidathineon, which eventually becomes such a hustling, congested street, begins in quiet contemplation outside the old but over-restored church of the **Metamorfosis tou Sotera**. The corner that it forms with Kodrou is a dumping place for rubbish and its low stone walls and benches are a temporary home to the homeless, a sanctuary for the lost. It is a sad little corner.

Turning away from the Acropolis up to the peaceful end of Kidathineon, and then left into Nikis (which eventually continues into Syntagma), the **Jewish Museum** is at number 39, just a short way up the street. It is a dark, dignified and enclosed building. Sadly, it has to be guarded and it is necessary to ring to enter, but it is both moving and fascinating to visit: a quiet, well-organized space with a superb collection. Before the Second World War there was a community of 78,000 Jews in Greece which had been settled there for 2,500 years. Fewer than 10,000 survived the Holocaust. Of these, many only did so because of a perhaps unique degree of protection and sympathy within the local population. **Archbishop Damaskinos** was the only religious leader in Europe to make an official protest against the deportations, also ordering his priests to issue fake baptismal certificates to conceal Jewish identity. Three thousand Jews now live in Athens.

Photographs, documents and diaries bear testimony to their predecessors' suffering and fate. But this museum is not only or even primarily a lament; its displays are an unusual and important reflection of the richness of the lives and rituals of the very different Jewish communities in Greece. A whole synagogue from Patras has been re-erected here and there are many cases of religious artefacts, but perhaps most appealing are the beautifully elaborate eighteenth- and nineteenth-century costumes and textiles with which Greek Jews once celebrated unique lives.

The **Frissiras Museum of Contemporary Art** is close by at Monis Asteriou, 3 & 7, a street running off Kidathineon to the east, a very short distance from the church, on the opposite side of the road. It houses some pieces by famous names – of non-Greeks, Paula Rego and Frank Auerbach are perhaps the best known – but it is the building itself that steals the show. Two flamboyant turreted late-neoclassical buildings in terracotta, gold and white contain galleries which are light and minimalist.

Returning to Kidathineon, between and above the shops are some substantial and attractive houses, mostly built in the late nineteenth and early twentieth centuries. Number 9 was once the home of the Nobel Prize-winning poet, George Seferis, and the **Museum of Greek Folk Arts** stands at 17. A young baker just on the corner of the little alley to the left runs his business on traditional lines, right down to the black-dressed *yiayia* – the ubiquitous and omnipotent Greek grandmama – presiding over the table outside. Almond croissants and bread, including the vast brown boulder that is the country loaf, come out of the oven early in the morning, followed by almost flat Greek pies: spinach, ham and cheese, flaky and melting straight from the oven and almost too hot to hold.

As it comes into the eastern side of Plateia Filomoussou Etairias, with its wall-to-wall cafés, kebab and ice-cream stands and importuning waiters, Kidathineon is crossed by Angelou Geronda. Just twenty metres in either direction, some authentic Greek food is being prepared for a largely local clientele in simplicity and peace and in surroundings which are among the most beautiful in Athens. *O Tristato* is to the far left. It is a small café with no such frills as umbrellas; you sit outside if the sun's rays are directed elsewhere. Inside it is very simple with high ceilings, faded pictures and lace curtains. Go there if only to eat Greek rice pudding – a very different affair from the insulating British variety. It is cold, light and smooth, with only the tiniest whole grains suspended in its creaminess; it is the Athenian antidote to an impossible day. *O Tristato* also serves tisanes in bamboo filters. Mixed mountain herbs look worryingly agricultural – straw, twigs and large leaves – but taste calming and fragrant.

At the very far end of the same street, *O Glikis*, at Angelou Geronda 2, has blue-painted chairs on an old paved terrace and small tables under a dense vine-covered pergola. It is the perfect place for lunch – the *poikilia* is a plate of *mezhedes* best accompanied by Macedonian white wine. In the evening *O Glikis* metamorphoses, almost unbelievably, from drowsy café to cosmopolitan urban bar.

Meanwhile its neighbour, slightly hidden up an alley, is a fragment of pre-war Athens. *Xinou* has sat in its large courtyard for ever. It is the centre of hostilities for every cat in Plaka and the screeches and thuds of animals falling off walls and leaping from one roof level to another are occasionally echoed in the sounds of human violence: helicopters, small-arms fire, bad-alien theme music, all emanating from the late show at the nearby rooftop open-air *Ciné Paris*.

Xinou is impervious to such dramas. Good, basic Greek dishes are served by old-time waiters. There are numerous variations on lamb, meatballs with spaghetti, sweet-flavoured cucumber-and-tomato salad, and fresh sardines. Or sometimes there is not. 'Bad' says the waiter succinctly, to a suggested choice of pork chops. 'Lamb is good.' There is only one option for pudding: Halva. Halva, in Greece, is a semolina-based cake, a sweet, slightly glutinous last challenge to the stomach. It is inescapable; most tavernas brandish it as a reward right at the end of an already excessive meal. It is generosity as test of endurance.

Even older than the waiters are the legendary *Xinou* trio. They are currently a duo but it seems bad form to notice. Both are well into their sixties or beyond. One is dark, thin and melancholy but the artist in him emerges in long green or red mod jackets and string ties. The other is a strong-looking, affable man in beige and grey polyester. The customers are, in the main, older still: well turned out Greek gentlemen in their eighties and their finely coiffed wives in flowered dresses. They have the pale waxy complexions of a life spent in the shade. In their lives they have seen Athens at its worst and at its best.

The trio, both of them, know what their audience likes and they give it to them night after night. Quite the oldest features of the restaurant are the songs: Greek ballads, mainly, and as the diners join in the choruses there are tears at some tables when the singers hit the rising phrase 'Athene, Athene'.

The **Ciné Paris** is at Kidathineon 22. Outside, film posters are for sale: *Star Wars*, *The Hours* or *Reservoir Dogs* become strangely desirable in Greek. Inside, an usherette in evening dress clips a ticket bought from a kiosk half a metre away. A stairway decorated with scenes from great movies emerges onto the roof. It is all very homely. Perhaps two dozen people at seats scattered round little tables. There is a balcony, even two little boxes, all under the stars and the treetops, with the lights of apartments to one side, the illuminated Acropolis to the other and the moon rising slowly. Byron would have loved it. A kitten mews for its mother in front of the screen, some television show can be heard drifting from open windows. The bar sells wine and nachos, the audience murmur, cuddle, put their feet on their tables, smoke and enjoy the film. All films are run in English with Greek subtitles but Athenian film preference seems to fall into three categories: farce (Italian or Greek), despair (French or Scandinavian) or psychopathic violence (usually imported from America). It is somehow irrelevant; the play's not the thing.

At 41 is **Vrettos**, Athens's oldest distillery. By day, a gloomy cave of ancient barrels racked one above another, with the occasional customer nursing his ouzo, silent in the darkness; by night, a polychrome grotto, a thousand bottles of liqueur standing floor to ceiling: purple, mandarin, delicate pink, amber, green, all lit from behind. These are displays which might have matched the Parthenon's gaudy colours in their prime if the Ancient Greeks had only known electricity. At *Vrettos* is every ouzo known to or forgotten by man.

Into the evening crush bursts a very large clown: his cropped hair is bleached, his ears are pierced, he wears a slaughterer's leather jerkin and carries long balloons. He is sweating heavily from a hundred balloon haloes, poodles and inflatable genitalia created in an evening for captive and embarrassed tourists. 'I want my lawyer,' he shouts, banging on the bar, then grins, flinging his arm around the owner. 'This man is my father and still he charges me for drink.' The more English of the drinkers smile with nervous relief. Street theatre is marginally better than naked violence.

In the dark basement underneath *Vrettos* is one of Athens's most famous single-feature enterprises. This enterprise is cod. Deep-fried cod with chips and garlic sauce is the pièce de résistance. Faced with the basement and the cod, the tourists and the heat, the owners close down between May and September. *O Damigos*, one of winter's comforts.

Amplified music on the street was banned a decade or so ago and many nightclubs closed down, but as you wander by each shop has its own gentle musical territory. It is not all what you might expect. Tosca at the top of Kidathineon, cello practice from a balcony door in Angelou Geronda, Vaughan Williams's *Fantasia on a Theme by Thomas Tallis* – loudly – in Dedalou.

At Adrianou 79 the neighbourhood fetish shop has cat-girl and cheeky S/M boy outfits on 1970s mannequins in windows adorned with chains looped like Christmas streamers. More testimonials. Rael, French cult leader, formerly a journalist called Claude and now an extraterrestrial ambassador, buys his ambassadorial uniform here. It is designed by Dimitris Souanatos. The manager (perhaps Souanatos himself?) sits smilingly outside the shop under a fig tree, dressed in black leather, crimson hair and rhinestone flesh. The temperature is forty degrees without the leather. He is listening to *Carmen*. Next door is the window of a shabby Greek costumiers. Dummies in dusty rayon Evzone skirts, something horribly flammable in vestal-virgin style, and boleros trimmed with gold ric-rac lurch against a faded crêpe-paper backcloth. It is all much creepier than Rael and the studded clubbers.

At number 88, near the turn to Mnisskleous, raw blank walls of neighbouring houses with air-conditioning units displayed like modern sculptures surround a small site where massive foundations are clearly exposed among the weeds. This is probably the location of the **Pantheon** of the Roman emperor Hadrian, whose library, only two minutes' walk away, and the arch and temple on Vassilissis Sofias, are Roman Athens's greatest surviving legacy and whose name is remembered in this street's designation. Less well served by fortune is the almost invisible Ottoman house, possibly the oldest dwelling in the city, which rots away at Adrianou 96.

Unless rescued it will undoubtedly soon collapse – a great loss to the record of architecture in Athens.

At 112 is *Kotsalis*. Dating from 1906, this is one of Athens's last surviving dairy cafés. Its walls are a museum of a life in milk. Serious games-mistress-like girls serve milk drinks, cakes and other wholesome patisserie and tubs of whipped cream. (The tubs are for decadents to take away.) *Kotsalis* is a cool and almost clinically ordered world. Here Athenian ladies immerse themselves in the quiet pleasure of *galaktobouriko* (baked custard in filo pastry topped with honey syrup), restrained lovers share milk shakes and a priest and his mother drink lemon tea.

A little further down the street, at number 129, the artist and sculptor Moraitis sits within his house and studio. He too is having a drink. The interior of this house of living quarters and workspace combined is a wonder: upstairs Moraitis's students chat and work, while downstairs the artist himself, an elegant man dressed in white, holds court

National costume shop

with his friends and a languid dog. Visitors move uncertainly around the paintings and his personal possessions, inhibited by this collision of private and public space. Eye contact is a problem. Step in to see the ceilings, the carvings and the neoclassical fantasy he has created as a background to his life and work.

Leave Plaka at its most dramatic boundary, following the curve of Adrianou westwards. In the evening the view is almost obliterated by the dazzling sun setting behind the ruins of **Hadrian's Library**. The café *Ydria*, in a little square with box hedges, leafy mulberry trees and sofas round a small rocky grotto, is opposite the tall and solid end-wall of this once-remarkable building. Cold chocolate or lemon tea seem in keeping with this green and shady spot.

The site is neither extensive nor (often) open, but the library's sunken position, surrounded by Areos, Dexipou and Eolou, means that it is almost better viewed from above. Walk around its edge: its courts and column bases, lecture theatre, garden, pool, the foundations of a church built later, even the niches that once held books can still be identified.

⬤

Hadrian constructed other buildings also for the Athenians: a temple of Hera and Zeus Panhellios, a sanctuary common to all the gods, and, most famous of all, a hundred pillars of Phrygian marble. The walls too are constructed of the same material as the cloisters. And there are rooms there adorned with a gilded roof and with alabaster stone, as well as with statues and paintings. In them are kept books.

Pausanias, second century CE

⬤

Turn left by the library and there is the **Roman Agora**, a quiet site in a wonderful position. The Acropolis rises behind it to the south, and the **Tower of the Winds** stands on its eastern boundary (see Introduction). The whole area takes its name – *Aerides* – from this small but unique monument.

It is not the only ancient building to have proved remarkably versatile. The Parthenon was, for a while, an arsenal, which proved – quite literally – to be its downfall; the Hephaeston became a church and then a storage facility; the Choregic Monument of Lysiscrates, absorbed into the monastery, was turned into a library. The Tower of the Winds was adopted as a baptistery by the Byzantine regime and in Ottoman times housed Dervishes who danced themselves into bleeding unconsciousness, much to the fastidious horror of Christian diary-writers. Under the nineteenth-century King Otto it housed a Catholic religious order. It has always been a source of speculation and puzzlement; over the centuries it has been believed to be the Prison of Socrates, a Temple of the God of the Winds and the tomb of Philip of Macedon.

The instruments sounding quicker, they kept time, calling out *Allah, Al illa All Allah*. God. There is no other God but God. Other sentences were added to these as their motion increased; and the chief Dervish bursting from the ring into the middle, as in a fit of enthusiasm, and letting down his hair behind, began turning about, his body poised on one of his great toes as a pivot, without changing place. He was followed by another, who spun a different way, and then by more, four or five in number. The rapidity, with which they whisked around, was gradually augmented and became amazing; their long hair not touching their shoulders but flying off; and the circle still surrounding them, shouting and

throwing their heads backwards and forwards; the
dome re-echoing the loud music; and the noise as it
were frantic Bacchanals.

Richard Chandler, 1765

This site is not large and to the north and west much of it
still disappears under houses, but the details of the Roman
market – small shops, an arcade, some marble paving and
drainage – have been clearly exposed by excavations. The
formal gate – a substantial Doric portico known as the Gate
of Athena Archegetes – is at the western end and an
inscription names Julius Caesar and his adopted son Augustus
as late first century BCE donors of this construction. An edict
by Hadrian controlling the trade in oil (and demonstrating
that his interventions in the city were not always merely
aesthetic) is on the north side. Another mundane but crucial
achievement and indicator of the level of business once
transacted at the Agora is the ruin of the once-magnificent
communal sixty-eight-seater latrine, to the right of the Tower
of the Winds.

From its noisy, smelly, bustling days as the commercial
centre of Roman Athens to its re-emergence as a place of
quiet and genteel reflection in the nineteenth century and on
into the twentieth, this has not always been a happy place.
The site was finally cleared of an ugly army bakery and the
camps housing refugees from the Asia Minor débâcle just
before the Second World War but there are still survivals from
troubled times on this site. To one end of the agora the
fifteenth-century **Fethiye – or Victory – Mosque**, dating from
the Ottoman occupation, is in good condition, although it is
currently closed. Diagonally opposite the Tower of the Winds,
behind scattered taverna tables, and covered with morning

Ruined Ottoman seminary

glory, is a more sinister ruin. Steps and an elaborate doorway were the entrance to a **Muslim Medresse**, or seminary. It later became a prison and Greeks were hanged from a tree in its courtyard. Nothing more than this fragment of façade endures; the uneven craters and hunks of stone that can be seen through the doors are the remains of a building which once inspired dread.

Walking up the eastern flank of the Tower of the Winds, the second small street to the left, Kiristou, is named after the astronomer and architect of the tower. A small diversion reveals another relic of the Turkish past, this time a delightful although little-known one. The Ottoman baths at Kiristou 8, which functioned from the 1600s to 1960, seemed destined for disintegration until recently. However, they have now been saved and restored and are currently open on Wednesdays. You could pass the building a hundred times and not identify it, yet, when you know what it is, its shape becomes obvious. The gloriously named **Bathhouse of the Winds** still has an interior that is a perfect relic of the days of Turkish domination and eastern architecture.

●

> The Consul's wife, Madame Gaspari, and I went into the room which precedes the bath, which room is the place where the women dress and undress, sitting like sailors upon boards: there were above fifty: some having their hair washed, others dyed, or plaited; some were at the last part of their toilet, putting with a fine gold pin, the black dye into their eyelids. In short, I saw here Turkish and Greek nature, through every degree of concealment, in her primitive state, for the women sitting in the inner room were so many Eves.
>
> Lady Elizabeth Craven, 1789

●

Plaka is one of very few places in Athens where the architectural legacy of the hated Turkish occupation is still visible. Much was torn down at the time of independence and subsequently in the rush to expose ancient sites, but unlike the remaining neoclassical architecture, which is largely being renovated, the legacy of the Ottoman empire continues to deteriorate.

Where Kiristou crosses Mnisskleous, turn left downhill and left again into the hushed street of traditional houses that is Diogenous. After a few metres this leads into a small square, almost entirely shaded by a great plane tree and home to one of Plaka's oldest restaurants: *O Platanos*. This is certainly no secret find (there are more visitors than local Greeks) but it makes few concessions to tourism.

This little backwater, so close to the busiest streets of Plaka, has a restful feel despite the occasional performances of R&B on an incongruous bazouki and amplifier by a busker who makes his pitch across the square. From the opposite side, gentler sounds occasionally carry on the breeze from the instruments of the **Museum of Greek Folk Music** at Diogenous 3. Here are lyres, dulcimers, *defi* (tambourines), bagpipes, lutes and guitars. Instructive, quaint, curious and beautiful, the history of each instrument is part of the heritage and culture of Greece.

These now little-seen instruments have symbolic as well as historical significance; music has always been a central part of regional and national identity, of celebration and of suffering. Summer recitals, music courses and recordings demonstrate the diversity of what was once a rich musical tradition but which now scarcely survives beyond the *laterna* players now largely performing for tourists. (The bazouki is the notable exception; music pounds from speeding cars in Athens, but it is more often a modern Greek sound than hip-hop or drum-and-bass.)

Behind *O Platanos*, the street returns again to the Tower of the Winds.

The boundary of the Agora is marked by bright cafés, blurring one into another and only distinguished by a change in tablecloth or umbrella colour. A corner table at *The Five Brothers* at Eolou 3 is as good as it gets and is surprisingly often available; this largely undiscovered spot has an uninterrupted view of the Agora under pink and white oleander bushes.

Walk straight on along the northern side of the Roman Agora along Pelopida and past the mosque, left into Panos, right into Epaminonda. Here more excavations can be seen clearly on the left-hand side; a small arcade of shops with colonnades, statue bases and steps is unmistakable in shape. The street, with a small temple in one of the units, once led from the ancient to the Roman Agora and was faced in marble.

A dog-leg into Pikilis is worth taking just to gaze across the ruins to a perfect nineteenth-century Athenian house. This stuccoed villa in deep ochre, a life-size statue in a niche in its façade, is stunningly situated at the foot of the Acropolis and half-hidden behind cypresses. It is actually situated at Polignotou 13 but, sadly, it is not accessible to the public. On a pale pink stucco wall in quiet Pikilis, more graffiti: 'Olympic Games. Game Over!' Turn right down Areos and Plateia Monastiraki, with its mosque and metro station, lies ahead.

THE SECOND WIND
South-West

Lips

*At the stern of a
swiftly-moving ship*

- The Boulevard of Dionissiou Areopagitou
- The ancient Theatre of Dionysos
- The Roman Theatre of Herodes Atticus
- The Acropolis
- The Hills of Philopappus, the Pnyx and the Areopagus
- The houses, shops and restaurants of Makrigiani

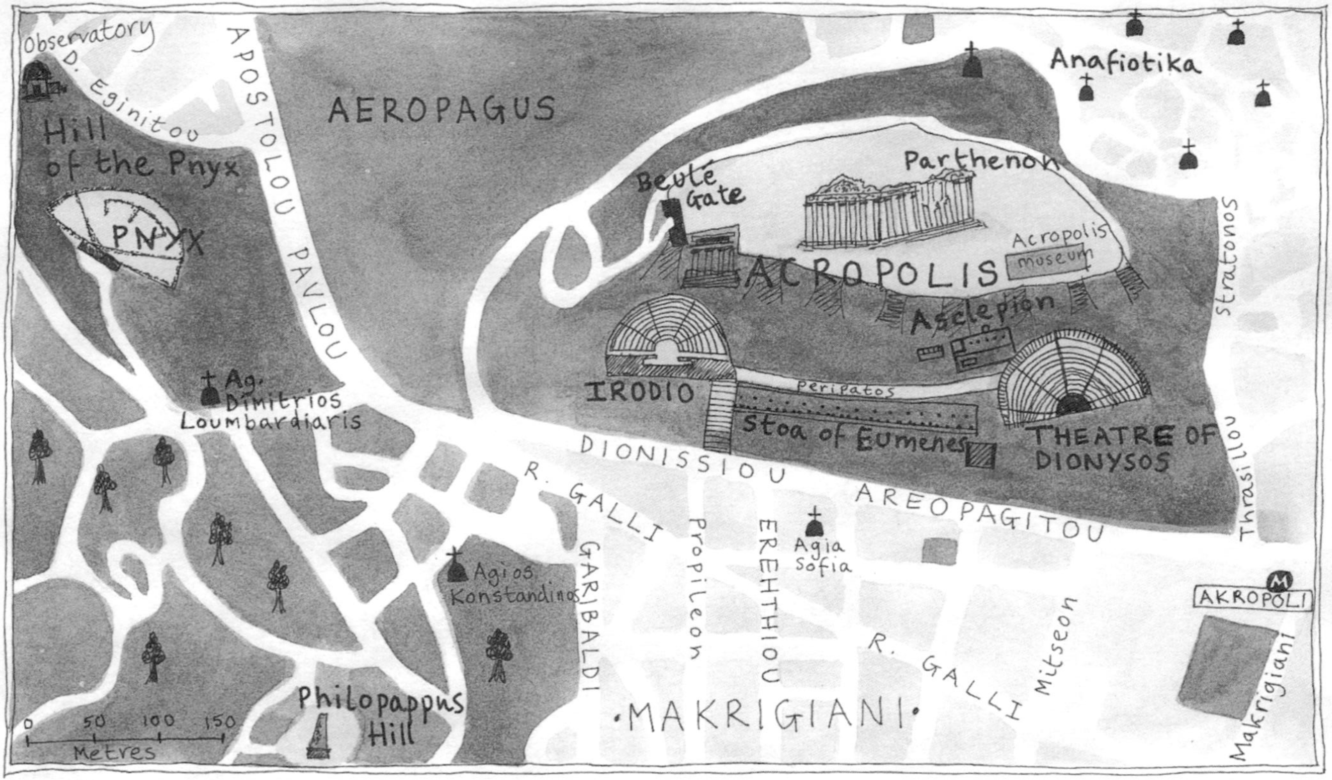

Observatory
D. Eginitou

AEROPAGUS

Anafiotika

Parthenon

Beule Gate

ACROPOLIS

Acropolis museum

Asclepion

Stratonos

Thrasillou

THEATRE OF DIONYSOS

Peripatos

IRODIO

Stoa of Eumenes

DIONISSIOU AREOPAGITOU

AKROPOLI

Makrigiani

Mitseon

R. GALLI

Agia Sofia

EREHTHIOU

Propileon

MAKRIGIANI.

R. GALLI

GARIBALDI

Agios Konstandino

APOSTOLOU PAVLOU

Hill of the Pnyx

Agi. Dimitrios Loumbardiaris

PNYX

Philopappus Hill

0   50   100   150
Metres

Irodio   Theatre of Herodes Attikus   Philopappus   Hills of the Muses

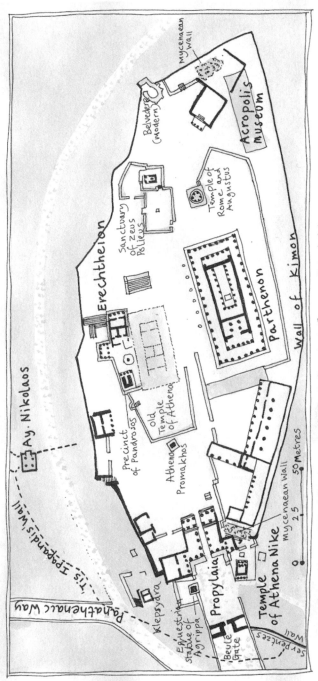

THE ACROPOLIS ~ PLAN

Ay. Nikolaos

Tis Ippapanis Wall

Panathenaic Way

Klepsydra

Equestrian Statue of Agrippa

Beulé Gate

Propylaia

Temple of Athena Nike

Serpentzes Wall

Mycenaean Wall

0 2 5 50 Metres

Athena Promakhos

old Temple of Athena

Precinct of Pandrosos

Erechtheion

Sanctuary of Zeus Polieus

Parthenon

Temple of Rome and Augustus

Belvedere (modern)

Mycenaean Wall

Acropolis Museum

Wall of Kimon

The Parthenon is the most famous and most famously inspiring monument in the Western world. Its fragments – stolen, bought, copied, faked – and its perceived ideals have travelled throughout most of the world to be tailored to local demand; no monument, no architectural convention has proved itself quite so adaptable to the aesthetic agendas of nations. From the Athens of the North – the chilly, empty monument on Calton Hill in Edinburgh – to the Athens of the South – a whole Parthenon (complete with marbles) in facsimile but on a gentler rise, to encourage less devoted or energetic visitors, in Nashville, Tennessee – from the temples of learning that are the national museums of the West to the celebration of power that is Capitol Hill, the Parthenon lives on.

Like religious relics, even fragments have the power to confer probity or gravitas or claims to a proper education. The dimensions, the architectural orders, the details of a column or capital or pediment are connections to a past and an ideology perceived as perfect. The Parthenon marbles are in replica inside the Akropolis metro station, confronting the tourist before the site is even reached. They are also, of course, in replica on the Parthenon itself, the originals famously and contentiously in the British Museum, as is one of the caryatids from the Erechtheion.

On a million keyrings, mugs and T-shirts, in plastic snowstorms, on ashtrays and place mats, the Parthenon is not just the symbol of Athens, in the way that the Eiffel Tower is of Paris, the Sydney Opera House is of Australia, or even the Colosseum is of Rome. It is the symbol of the whole of classical antiquity; and, by extension, of the values of democracy, art and knowledge.

The caryatids too have made long journeys west, bearing the burdens of banks, shops and bourgeois balconies. Pristine in restoration at the Ziller house in Assomaton; neglected,

broken and recently fallen at another Ziller house in
Mavromihali; sooty and patient in the Euston Road, London;
hefty and white between the shops of Montpellier,
Cheltenham, exemplars of civic solidity for the members of
the adjacent Ladies' College.

Until up there detached from her ruins she appeared
    gaining in
Height and beautiful beyond addition with all the
    birds' habits in
Her sway daughter the north wind was bringing and
    I waiting

Each fathom forward as she flung a small breast to
    resist the wind
And from me a terrified happiness raising its wing
    to my lids

Ai! Tempers and madness of my land!

Odysseas Elytis, b. 1911:
'Daughter the North Wind Was Bringing'

The Acropolis can be reached either by taking the more
eccentric path through Plaka and Anafiotika, with the
advantage of views over the ancient *agora*, or up the more
formal approach of Dionissiou Areopagitou. The Akropolis
metro is just minutes away. The conversion of Dionissiou
Areopagitou to a pedestrian boulevard has been one of the
great successes of the last ten years. It is already incorporated
into the traditional pleasures of Athenian life. At night
couples and families wander up its broad space, children play
football, a classical trio or a lone guitarist echoes the large-

Akropolis metro station

scale productions in the Theatre of Herodes Atticus. Food-stall snackers and tourists in shorts mingle with opera-goers, elegant in silk and linen. Handsome houses follow the gradual incline to the left and on the other side a promenade under the trees gives both access to and fine views of the Theatres of Dionysos and of Herodes Atticus tucked in at the base of the Acropolis.

The two theatres are survivals of quite different periods of prosperity in Athens's past. The site of the **Theatre of Dionysos** is at the bottom of Dionissiou Areopagitou, the entrance on the corner with Thrasillou street. Here are terraces of scattered masonry, columns, a tiny chapel and olive trees. Among the scree and the little paths are the clear outlines of long-gone buildings. Birds nest under the cliff of the Acropolis, and there are occasional reluctant tortoises in cool crevices under the marble. It was not always so peaceful. It was here that drama first evolved out of rites to the god Dionysos. The new art unfolded astonishingly fast; from the first play by Thespis in 543 BCE to Aeschylus' completion of the *Oresteia* trilogy was a matter of some seventy-five years. Two thousand five hundred years later the *Oresteia* is still performed.

Every March the Festival of Dionysia was celebrated in music and literature with competitions between writers of comedy and tragedy. It was in this place that the plays of Aeschylus, Aristophanes, Euripides and Sophocles were first performed and attracted audiences from the city and overseas; in time productions toured to other cities. The Theatre of Dionysos was altered many times but the remains visible today are, broadly, from the fourth century BCE with many later additions.

The auditorium still has twenty-five of its original seventy-eight closely packed rows of seats built of limestone. In the first row are the thrones for the great and good, carved in Pentelic marble, some with lion's-paw feet and still evocatively inscribed with their original occupant's name; the finest once belonged to the High Priest of Dionysos. The images seen in the ironwork and carvings of the nineteenth-century houses in the area have their precursors here: satyrs, grapes, winged figures and griffins.

Above the theatre is a cave in the rock face of the Acropolis. This was once a shrine to Dionysos but it is now a strange and atmospheric little chapel, currently closed to the public, whose darkness and fading frescos hardly match the expectations that its name **Panayia Hrissospiliotissa** (Our Lady of the Golden Cave) inspires. It is still unequivocally a pagan place.

To the left a quiet terrace stretches between cypress trees; there is little in the ruins here that is instantly identifiable but this peaceful place was once the **Asclepion**, a temple of healing where sufferers would sacrifice to the god, wash in a sacred spring, be treated by priestly healers and then sleep in the hope of effecting a cure. It is not so very far from the treatments of today. The cult was brought from Epidavros to Athens in 329 BCE, when the city was afflicted with the plague. There were sacred serpents in the temple whose images survive today as symbols on the staff of Asclepius used by the medical profession. Lovers of symbolism explain that a snake sloughs off its skin and is renewed (though a less elevated but more probable explanation is that early doctors used to extract the endemic parasitical guinea worms through slits in their patients' skin by coiling the parasites round a stick). The serpents also survive on the ground (they are classified as *elaphe longissima*) and are found in their original habitats in southern Europe but also further north where Asclepions were established in antiquity. Asclepius was the father of medicine, as well as of Meditrina, Hygeia and Panacea, his daughters, and his temples were the precursors of medical schools.

The **Theatre of Herodes Atticus** (with a separate access off Dionissiou Areopagitou) is a very different structure from that of Dionysos and from a very different time. It was erected in the second century CE, when Athens was flourishing under Roman protection. Herodes Atticus was an immensely wealthy Roman senator and he gave this theatre to the city in memory of his wife Regilla. What has been restored today is still imposing. Up to three storeys of the arched façade survive and the interior can best be seen from above on the Acropolis.

During the Athens Festival from June to September concerts and opera are staged here. The rows of stone tiers are narrow and hard – the thin cushions are a gesture, not proper upholstery. The strings have to retune frequently in the heat. At nine, the orchestra enters, formal but jacketless, and the echoing babble of talk dies away to silence. The temperature can still be eighty degrees. The conductor lifts his arms, wearing a silk shirt so thin that it billows, transparent, in the stage lights, while the chorus enters, courageous in wigs and make-up and brocaded gowns. Herodes Atticus' cedar roof, an engineering marvel in its day, is long gone; the sky turns violet, then the first stars come out, pigeons grumble in the niches and bats occasionally swoop into the spotlight, some dogs bark and a distant car races down the street.

The cast and audience spill out into Dionissiou Areopagitou close on midnight. There are, inevitably, some good restaurants in the area ready to feed them. *Symbosio*, at Erehthiou 46, is a sophisticated choice. Set in the courtyard of a beautifully restored 1920s house, the food is exceptional, the service flawless. Wild boar, swordfish, milk-fed lamb and wild asparagus are among many seasonal choices. *Strofi* is at the opposite end of the spectrum. A very ordinary-looking house at Rovertou Galli 25, it produces excellent traditional food in a friendly taverna and is frequented by the spear-carriers and clarinettists of Herodes Atticus at the end of hot evenings. It also has its own theatrical view of the Acropolis from its rooftop.

In many ways the impact of the Acropolis is greater when seen from afar. The Parthenon sits above the city, outside its concerns, flawless, unreal and detached. Closer to, some of that magical perfection disappears. J.P. Mahaffy, a nineteenth-century Irish academic, concluded that such is its legacy to the collective imagination that it cannot fail to disappoint. It is perhaps that there is nothing left to think about the edifice: it has all been thought.

In high season it is the lack of time or perspective to react at all that is the problem. The rock acts as a radiator and columns of visitors from every country in the world, girded about with cameras, sunhats and paper parasols, their *Blue Guides* or *Baedekers* or even, occasionally, a copy of Pausanias wind snakelike to the entrance. They stand, trying to get a clear view or shot of their heritage in a dense, slightly awed crowd or sit hot and bewildered in any shade that they can find. Great cranes tower over the scene, hunks of clean stone lie numbered and tidy, the army of restoration moves across the pediments or brushes diligently at a step. The project to repair the repairs of the nineteenth century which have, in the dilapidation that they have caused, done so much to damage the structures, will take years.

●

The distant appearance of the Acropolis somewhat resembles that of Stirling Castle, but is inferior in altitude and general effect.

John Galt, writing in 1809–11

●

Yet although the modern visitor may be too inhibited by the crowd to be moved to tears, as Cyril Connolly claimed to be, the temples of the Acropolis remain impressive. Their beauty survives – just – the crush of admirers, the buzz of wonder, the technology of care. The current entrance, via the Beulé Gate, provides a dizzying perspective of the monument: the tiny Temple of Athena Nike is exquisite and the Erechtheion with its Caryatids petrified in eternal lapidescence is, quite simply, a wonder. This is the building most often recalled with delight by visitors.

The vantage point over Athens from the eastern belvedere of the Acropolis is spectacular. Go early or late to avoid the worst of the heat and the people. Weeping might come more easily and more privately in the dark; the site is occasionally and delightfully opened on a summer's night so that the ruins can be seen at their romantic best by moonlight.

– 'Listen. There's this too. In the moonlight
the statues sometimes bend like reeds
in the midst of ripe fruit – the statues;
and the flame becomes a cool oleander,
the flame that burns one, I mean.'

– 'It's just the light . . . shadows of the night.'

– 'Maybe the night that split open, a blue
    pomegranate,
a dark breast, and you filled with stars,
cleaving time.
               And yet the statues
Bend sometimes, dividing desire in two,
Like a peach; and the flame
Becomes a kiss on the limbs, then a sob,
Then a cool leaf carried off by the wind;
They bend; they become light with a
   human weight.
You don't forget it.'

George Seferis, 'Thrush', 1946

The Erechtheion was once a museum of sorts; as well as a temple it contained, and gave visitors the chance to revere, various historical curiosities. It also housed a fortunate sacred snake fed on honey cakes. There was a folding chair made by Daedalus and battle spoils from Persian conflicts: the gold plaques of the armoured vest of the commander of Xerxes' army; the sword of Mardonius, son-in-law of Darius; an olive-wood statue of Athena Polias.

    The Acropolis Museum could be seen in the same spirit. It will eventually move down to a site on the other side of Dionissiou Areopagitou. For the time being it is up here telling the story of the ruins and displaying some of their finest exhibits (including the caryatids, which have been replaced by replicas on the site itself). Room IV is perhaps the most moving. Here are the *korai*, statuettes often holding animals or fruit and designed as gifts for the gods. After they were damaged in the Persian attack of the fifth century BCE, the Athenians buried these precious objects and they stayed interred for more than two thousand years until, still showing marks of the catastrophe that felled them, they were excavated by archaeologists. Some of the archaeological finds are in the National Museum but this is a collection that is best seen within the immediacy of its context.

An illiterate servant of the Disdar of Athens ... assured me that when the five (other) maidens had lost their sister, they manifested their affliction by filling the air at close of the evening with the most mournful cries and lamentations, that he himself had heard their complaints, and never without being so much affected that he had to leave the citadel until they had ceased; and the ravished sister was not deaf to their voice, but astonished the lower town where she was placed by answering in the same lamentable tones.

F.S.N. Douglas: *On the Removal of a Caryatid from the Erechtheion*, 1802

Adjacent to the Acropolis is the low hill of the **Areopagus** (see Walk 3), which can be reached by a treacherous flight of ancient steps. On rainy days these are potentially lethal and the hill where St Paul preached is itself a barren outcrop of rock, with a flattened plateau on top.

Back at the roadside entrance to the Acropolis is *Dionysos Restaurant*. It is also now the location of the famous *Zonar's Café*, which held court for years in faded magnificence in Syntagma Square. The location is superb and the prices reflect this. The food is good but the long modern building, the regularity of the outside terraces and, above all, the ranks of coaches and *Dionysos*'s own catering vans parked outside give it all a faint air of an upmarket motorway café. It is hard not to regret the lost art-deco rooms and the established Athenian clientele of *Zonar*'s previous life.

Beyond this point Rovertou Galli and Dionissiou Areopagitou join and become Apostolou Pavlou, descending slowly along the side of the Areopagus and then passing to the south-west of the ancient *agora* until it comes into Thissio (see Walk 3). On the left-hand side, the road forks uphill through the olive groves to the **Hill of the Muses** (better known as **Philopappus**), the **Nymphs** and the **Pnyx**. For anyone tired of the noise and frustrations of Athens, these provide glorious walks through countryside almost unchanged since antiquity and with some compelling classical connections. It is one of the few places in the city where the hum of cicadas can be clearly heard, where wild flowers and small animals flourish, and paths criss-cross the slopes in natural dappled light.

The story of Athens is in many ways a story of architects. The ruins of classical Athens have provided the enduring paradigm for architecture across the western world since its great flowering in the fifth century BCE. It was a reflection of eighteenth- and nineteenth-century fascination with all things antique, interest in the wake of early archaeological exploration and the Grand Tour that led to neoclassicism being reintroduced here from the outside. That no indigenous architect has emerged in the last century to equal earlier ones in fame is perhaps because of the cultural, aesthetic and historical burden of the distant past. The best modern Greek architecture has been in the realm of the private domestic house, not in public works.

Yet there is one architect who is the hero of twentieth-century design. He is a man whose work, using his own students and artists from the local community, resolves all the contradictions of preserving and displaying ancient monuments, of balancing the needs of the local community and of visitors and of looking to the future while preserving the spirit of the past. His projects are seen by thousands every year, yet their beauty and brilliance lies in their unobtrusiveness.

In the early 1950s, when Greece was only starting to recover from the war, **Dimitris Pikionis** began a project to connect the ancient monuments. His marble paths that wind up to the Acropolis follow ancient tracks and were deliberately set unevenly, using reclaimed irregular stone, to create an access route that feels as if it had always been there. Given a freer hand and less formal surroundings in the hills to the west of the Acropolis, Pikionis created a pretty, witty bricolage of antiquity. It grew from a creative impulse of affection without paralysis in the face of Athens's heritage. Slivers of marble and brick decorate paved tracks. Between the trees – all species known since antiquity – are watercourses, tiny mosaics, pictures in stone: a fish skeleton, a zodiac, a star. Shallow steps, low-walled belvederes and stone benches in small clearings blend with the remains of ancient fortifications.

Before the birth of the Muses, cicadas were human beings. When the Muses were born and song came into the world, some of the men of that age were so ravished by its sweetness that in their devotion to singing they took no thought to eat and drink, and actually died before they knew what was happening to them. From them sprang the race of cicadas, to whom the Muses granted the privilege that they should need no food but should sing from the moment of their birth till death without eating or drinking.

Plato: *Phaedrus*

The small church of **Ag. Dimitrios Loumbardiaris** lies on the left about 100 metres along the narrow road of the same name, leading between the Hills of the Muses and the Pnyx. Dating from the sixteenth century, the church acquired its name when a miracle was attributed to its patron saint. A Turkish cannon on the point of firing from the Acropolis onto the church was struck by lightning (*loumbardha* means cannon) and disabled. Pikionis restored the building with his customary imaginative touch and added a courtyard, benches and eating area. Half hidden in a grove of trees its

Ag. Dimitrios Loumbardiaris

story, its location, its appearance and spirit are all the stuff of magical fantasy. Opposite, the paths climb to the top of Philopappus where in Lent carnival kites swoop and fall as Athenians celebrate the festival in the spring breeze.

Generally the hills are best climbed in the early morning. They are often comply empty and pleasantly cool. The contrast between greater Athens distantly rumbling into another day, and the clouds of butterflies and birds that rise at a single footstep on the path, is marked then. However, it is at sunset that Philopappus is truly transfigured. The rocky peak, almost 150 metres above the city, provides one of the finest views of Athens and is an intensely dramatic spot.

On the crest of the hill is the monument to **Julius Philopappus**, an Athenian consul, Roman senator and last and exiled king of the vanished kingdom of Commagene. He was a man of immense wealth and influence, a close friend of the Emperor Hadrian. His once-splendid tomb, its tall, broken and curved façade still distinctive above the city, was probably erected by his sister Julia Balbilla in around 115 CE. It is an unrivalled spot. To the south-west the city ends in a vast expanse of sea, the source of Athenian trade and wealth and much closer than seems possible. To the west are the mountains, tipped with snow in winter, that enclose the city. Close at hand and a little dwarfed by the perspective is the Acropolis, symbol of religious power. The site of Philoppapus' tomb encompasses them all.

As the sun falls behind the mountains, it is very quiet up here: a wind flickers in the dried grass, a few people wait to see a spectacle that has remained the same for ever. A handful of dogs, apparently ownerless, appear from the bushes. From below, a saxophonist's notes carry clearly from the built-up streets to the empty hillside, and almost simultaneously with the sun going down the lights of Athens flicker on. The dogs begin a frantic barking and then Philopappus is left in darkness above the illuminated city he once loved.

●

> The little state of Kommagene, which flickered out
>   like a small lamp,
> Often comes to mind.

George Seferis: *Last Stop*

●

On the right-hand side of Ag. Loumbardiaris, with access up a path behind the church, lies the **Pnyx**; a site of huge significance in the history of Athens and of the Western world yet one little known beyond the *son et lumière* performances that are conducted here now. Following any one of a number of gentle paths to the top between thickets and trees, with only the occasional remnant of old building or wall, it is also hard to imagine this as the densely occupied area it was in classical Athens and which gave its name to the hill: *pyknos* – crowded, bustling with the mob.

Yet this was the birthplace of democracy. At the end of the sixth century BCE Kleisthenes introduced this new form of government and, leaving the pre-democracy meeting place in the *agora*, the Athenians climbed this hill to build an assembly overlooking their city. Here the great orators Pericles, Aristides and Themistocles addressed their audiences, here decisions which made, and eventually lost, an empire were taken. Not a lot remains of the structures of this time, but the Pnyx itself has been clearly identified and is recognizable in a terrace, residual steps and containing wall, a little below the summit to the north-west. It has a still and serious air.

From this part of the Pnyx the Acropolis is in immediate view. Although always distinctive and immediately recognizable, the Acropolis changes subtly in its relationship

The Pnyx

with Athens depending on where it is viewed from. From the Pnyx, looking across the Areopagus, the Acropolis seems very immediate, almost ziggurat-like, a flight of long steps covered with small dark figures who move up and down to the portico at the top.

Is this the renowned Athens? How melancholy would be the reflection should we suppose, what certainly must come to pass, that in a few ages hence, London, the Carthage, the Memphis, the Athens of the present world, be reduced to a state like this and travellers come perhaps from *America* to view its ruins.

Lord Charlemont, 1749

The Hill of the Nymphs – not, sadly, its ancient name but a felicitous nineteenth-century addition – to the north of the Pnyx is distinguished by its **observatory** designed by Hansen in 1847. It is closed to the public but is an attractive landmark on this pretty, fertile hill.

At this point it is just a short walk to rejoin Apostolou Pavlou and descend to Thissio and the metro. Alternatively, retrace the road back to where the road forks into Dionissiou Areopagitou and Rovertou Galli at a point just outside the *Dionysos* restaurant. The right-hand road runs parallel to and below the main boulevard.

This area, a dignified, unspoiled residential part of Athens, which is becoming better known as braver visitors penetrate the streets around the Acropolis, is known as **Makrigiani**. The town houses here are largely from the 1920s, the keystones over the door usually depicting a very severe Athena. Terraces of houses are interrupted by occasional excavation pits; some good restaurants and some well-placed hotels are appearing without changing the air of faded residential gentility. It is a pleasant way back to the Akropolis metro.

There are several shops selling small antiques around Makrigiani. They are all, in their way, small museums. Fortunately the owners tolerate browsers with equanimity. Heavy lace, bobbins, ivories, silver brushes, textiles and woven rugs lie in tumbled heaps. But this is no flea market: the owners know the value of every item and every tourist. A corner shop, opposite the newly restored Herodian hotel, has a window full of the felt and feather hats of the 1940s. *La Maison d'Antiquités* at Rovertou Galli 1 has old textiles, some darkly beautiful lamps and carved beds made up enticingly in heavy linen, cream with age, crocheted bedspreads with cherubs and garlands of flowers, and blankets from the chilly mountains. *Skyros*, as the name suggests, is rich with folk art, oil lamps and embroideries from the islands.

Another museum piece usually sits on the street at Rovertou Galli 21, just before the antique shops. This is the home of Mr Costas Stavropoulos. Outside, parked in the street among the Fiats and the Nissans, is his bright blue Mercedes. It is a local celebrity; stop and look at it and the *periptero* owner shouts for Mr Stavropoulos to come out. The car was first registered in 1940. Mr Stavropoulos was born twenty years or so earlier; both have acquired dignity with age. An English-speaking neighbour comes out of her shop. The car, she explains, was brought to Athens by the occupying Nazis. When Athens was liberated by the Allies, the Mercedes was found crated up at Piraeus, about to accompany its then owner on a long, one-way voyage to South America. Mr Stavropoulos acquired it instead, and it has remained in Athens ever since, fully taxed and used every day (there are some interesting lacunae in this story but it seems unmannerly to enquire). However, recently there have been fewer journeys. The shopkeeper shrugs: 'He is old man, it is old car, together now is not so good.'

Where Rovertou Galli comes into Makrigiani, turn left. The Akropolis metro is just up the street on the left. Opposite it are a handful of small shops and galleries. At Makrigiani 5, a husband and wife own the *Vergina* gallery and a small shop that provides information on the young artists and craftsmen whose work they display and sell. The work is fresh, understated and beautifully made. Yet behind many of the abstract designs there still hovers the shadow of the past: some ghost columns in a modern collage, a Greek key on enamelled silver earrings. A less sophisticated shop lies in a small side street, selling lurid replicas and resin busts of Aeschylus and Homer. It has an English name: *Giftshop The Very*. As with the Acropolis, there is ultimately a limiting nature to superlatives.

THE THIRD WIND
West

Zephyros

A young man, lightly clothed and scattering flowers from his lap

- The cafés, restaurants and traders of Thissio
- Athens's oldest railway line
- The Temple of Hephaestus
- The Ancient Agora
- The Pil-Poul hat factory/Melina Mercouri Cultural Centre

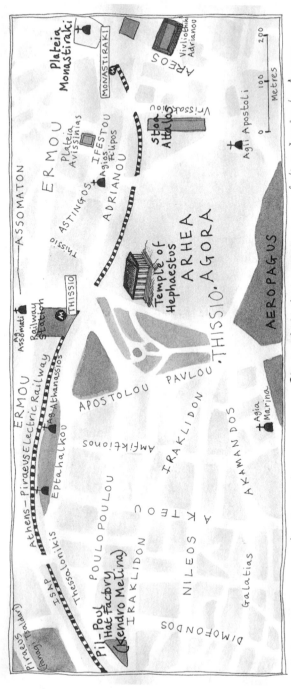

Arhea Agora   Ancient Agora   Stoa Attalos   Museum of the Ancient Agora
Kendro Melina   Melina Mercouri Cultural Centre   Vivliothiki Adrianou Hadrian's Library

Adrianou runs in a curve from Plaka to Thissio. It begins a short distance from the Arch of Hadrian, the Roman emperor whose name it bears. From Plateia Filomoussou Etairias (Place of the Lovers of the Arts) the café-filled square that lies at the heart of Athens's densest, but still appealing, tourist district; it cuts through the city's oldest inhabited area before it follows the periphery of the Roman Agora. At Monastiraki, when most other thoroughfares narrow and darken as they are drawn into the flea market, Adrianou widens into a charming boulevard following the old Piraeus railway line. Thissio marked the city limits for thousands of years and here Adrianou comes to a sudden end, confronted with relative modernity in the shape of the railway station and the fourteenth-century church, Ag. Assomati.

The character of Thissio is suspended between this railway station and the magnificent Doric temple to Hephaestus. The appeal of one is in its ordinariness, the other in its exceptional beauty.

For a long time the temple was known as the Thesion in the belief that it was the burial place of the bones of Theseus, founder of Athens, and it gave its name to the area around it. It was later re-identified as a fifth-century BCE temple, the largest in Greece, dedicated to the god of fire, of blacksmiths and of craftsmen. His bellows still blow; Thissio always seems slightly hotter than the rest of the city and the daytime stillness is broken by gusts that ruffle the leaves of small trees and send paper scratching down the street; earth crumbles around the pits where archaeologists still toil. It remains a place of sparks: of metal workshops, of the electric railway lines stretching on towards Piraeus, of the vicious battles fought on its streets only sixty years ago and of the temple to the industrial age at Gazi, where the skeletons of the gasworks that dominate the western city skyline as the

Hephaeston does the south-west are also relics to the needs and dreams of another age.

> ... By the street of Athena, head bent in thought, to the street of Hermes, where he loitered as if in uncertainty, indifference leading him at length to the broad sunshine of that dusty desolate spot where stands the Temple of Theseus. So nearly perfect that it can scarce be called a ruin, there, on the ragged fringe of Athens, hard by the station of the Piraeus Railway, its marble majesty consecrates the ravaged soil. A sanctuary still, so old, so wondrous in its isolation, that all the life of to-day around it seems a futility and an impertinence.

George Gissing: *Sleeping Fires*, 1895

To immerse yourself in the mood of the area it is best to approach on foot from **Monastiraki** rather than take a train as far as Thissio station. Turning right out of Monastiraki metro, this final segment of Adrianou is the first turning on the right, almost immediately opposite the still imposing western wall of Hadrian's great library.

Adrianou runs parallel with Ifestou. Ifestou is a dark, claustrophobic artery of the flea market, dense with people; Adrianou, as it sweeps down to Thissio, is sunlit and broad, with small tables set in the shade of trees and umbrellas. It is an ideal place for a slow walk or a long drink. Café tables abut the railings by the railway line; there is a whisper of breeze in the long dry grasses around ruins that tumble down to the track, and the trains rumble gently through. At the *Attalos* restaurant you can watch the trains and the ruins and the butterflies while lingering over *atomiko poikilia* – a largely fish-based *mezhede* for one – or grilled 'pleurotous' mushrooms, or spinach croquettes.

To the left are a stretch of pink and ochre neoclassical

houses, the clear lines of their ornamental eaves blurred by the nests of house martins. To the right, on the far side of the railway line, are the ruins of the **Ancient Agora**, for thirty-six centuries the heart of Athenian life. It has not always been as exposed and idyllic as it is today; for centuries Athens built over its ancient centre and when the vogue for archaeology took hold from the mid-nineteenth century onward, nearly 400 dwellings were demolished to reveal the foundations of the Greek world.

There is an entrance to the *agora* off Adrianou over a footbridge, another off Apostolou Pavlou to the south and it can also be reached straight from the Roman Agora. In fact, the successful linking of most of Athens's major sites into a single archaeological park means that for the energetic a wonderful walk from the foot of the Acropolis to the

Neoclassical house

Hephaeston is possible. Best undertaken in early morning or in the evening, the path descends through a beautiful and atmospheric landscape where tiny fragments of carving or unidentified crevices and pillars are almost more appealing than the ruins of more famous temples and theatres.

●

... Our abode is the nearest building to the Temple of Theseus on the extreme edge of the modern town. There are few other buildings near it. At a little distance to the south a peasant is now engaged in ploughing the earth with a team of oxen: the soil along which he is driving his furrows was once a part of the agora of Athens.

Christopher Wordsworth, 1832–3

●

The Ancient Agora covers a large area, its (ongoing) excavations interspersed with cypress trees and thickets of flowering oleander. Paths between the ruins encourage visitors to ramble at will: fallen masonry, culverts, statues and the knotted trunks of olive trees allow the imagination to take flight, unconstrained by the demands of historical reality. The one exception is the **Stoa of Attalos**, adjacent to Adrianou and on the north-western end of the site. This reconstruction of a second century BCE arcade of shops was undertaken by the American School of Archaeology in 1956. Its recreation, though well achieved, was not well received: it ran counter to the conventions against archaeological rebuilding. Its size, in an area of ruins, tended to dominate the site, reducing the visual impact of the Hephaeston. Having justified the project on grounds of authenticity the Americans rejected a restoration of the original blue and red paint, insisting that their pristine version was true to the authentic *ideal* of antiquity prevailing now if not in the past.

Maturation of the landscape has perhaps diminished the Stoa's over-powerful impact. It now houses the **Museum of the Ancient Agora** with finds from the Neolithic period right through to the sixth century CE when the city centre was finally destroyed in successive raids by the Visigoths and the Slavs. Here the ruins can be understood and unravelled. What is striking about the Stoa is not its solitary completeness in a city of ruins but that its architectural descendants flourish throughout Athens and, indeed, numerous other Mediterranean cities and towns: the arcade design has never been bettered for the running of small businesses in a country with hot summers and wet winters.

The Temple of Hephaestus or Hephaeston, raised above the *agora* on its knoll, has overlooked the changing market place for two and a half thousand years. There was always a garden on the site and the present species – olives, pomegranates and myrtle – were all grown in antiquity. The Hephaeston has had many subsequent lives, becoming a Christian basilica in the seventh century, an architectural conversion – generally a fortunate turn of fate for pagan buildings (though not, perhaps, for the gods themselves) as it usually ensured the structures' preservation. Inside – where access is intermittent – the British have left their mark: there are eighteenth- and nineteenth-century British tombs and some enduring British graffiti. The temple of the fire-wielding blacksmith was recast as the church of St George, slayer of the fire-breathing dragon, and functioned as such within the lifetime of Athenians still living. In 1834 the *Te Deum* was sung here to celebrate the arrival of the newly created Greek king Otto in the capital and it was performed again on the centenary of this service in 1934.

Just a decade later the peaceful temple, which had seen so

many conflicts and incursions, was a landmark in bloody inter-factional street fighting as the horrors and partisanship of the Second World War evolved into the most vengeful of civil wars.

●

There were the Panoliascu brothers holed up by Kerameikos, and the Papageorgiou band which operated in Pankrati. Colonel Grivas, who would become better known in the 1950s as leader of the EOKA movement in Cyprus, headed an underground royalist organization called 'X', which had started fighting the Germans but by 1944 was spending more time in clashes with the EAM from its bastion in the Thesion area beneath the Acropolis. In the side streets below the Thesion temple, 'X' gunmen exchanged shots with ELAS patrols.

Mark Mazower: *Inside Hitler's Greece* (1995)

●

Thissio is on the way up again. Restoration, pedestrianization and the cessation of its heavier, smellier industries have encouraged the return of smarter cafés and restaurants. Government money has paid for improvements to the best houses. Yet Athens has always defied zoning and in Thissio streets move from elegance to shabby neglect in the space of one block. In Odos Thissio, the shopfronts are stacked with cages of busy yellow and blue linnets. Beneath them plump brown rabbits sleep in their hutches unperturbed by the close observation of local cats. In an Adrianou overspill from the flea-market stalls of **Plateia Avissinias**, trinkets, playing cards and telephone cards are sold from small tables. The poorest vendors sit cross-legged beside a few well-used possessions: a pair of shoes so shaped by their previous owner that is hard to believe anyone else could wear them, a toy car, old framed photographs, some curtains – somebody's life.

But a few metres away, at Adrianou 7, it is quite a different story. The handsome Vassilissis Korovezes also has an outdoor table on which are an irresistible selection of old postcards: views of a strangely empty, strangely coloured turn-of-the-century Athens, fuzzy black-and-white poses of Independence heroes (one *Kapitan* Leonidas is armed, and whiskered, to the teeth), soft-focus ample French nudes and some tinted classical tableaux, all blushing flesh,

Civil War poster, flea market

wreaths and artful draperies. The real gems are inside where all is understated affluence. (This time the accompaniment is *Il Trittico*, but it is always Callas.) Here are early leather-bound guides to Greece, journals, contemporary English and French newspaper accounts of life in nineteenth-century Athens, even the personal photograph albums of hopeful travellers in the last years before the Second World War. Mr Korovezes has some handsome engravings of Athens too and, rarer, a stereoscope with numerous views of Greece. He endures the amusement that all this gives the most casual of shoppers with good humour.

On most days of the week an affable old man lurks in or outside Mr Korovezes's shop. He is a jolly Ancient Mariner, waiting for foreigners in need of a handshake and a story. His tale, which moves seamlessly and at gathering speed from Athens to Korea to the Front (unspecified) and from Greek to German to English and back, with some relief, to Greek, concerns Turkish fatalities, American hesitance and Hellenic courage. It is an illustrated talk; here in his wallet is a photograph of a much, much younger man at a gun emplacement. The edges are eroded and the cracks snake across the image; it will soon be hard to identify either the warrior or his war.

For a while between its ancient and modern industrial ages, Thissio was a gracious residential area. On the edge of town nearest the port of Piraeus, with fine views of the Acropolis, it was a location of choice for the merchants building impressive establishments to fit their rising status.

The confident church of **Ag. Filipos** midway down the street served this comfortable community. Beyond it is an extensive area of archaeological excavation; any repairs or demolition in such historically complicated ground inevitably expose more ruins and diggers negotiate planks and umbrellas balanced over deep cuttings and massive subterranean foundations. The rediscovery of Athens has been going on for one and a half centuries and looks set to continue to the end of time. What is being uncovered here are arcades of the north-west corner of the *agora*.

The house at Adrianou 3, as the street comes to an end, is one of the finest in the area. But, like so much in Athens, it has had a history of mixed fortunes and changing roles. It was built sometime around the 1890s for a distiller, Andreas Cambas. The family lived in some grandeur on the top floors while the basement was the bottling and storage plant and the ground floor housed Cambas's extensive wine cellar. He sold out to a louche cigarette heir but the house declined with the area as fumes from the factories at Gazi and the local settlement of refugees from Asia Minor made life less agreeable. From 1942 the building was commandeered by the Italians as a barracks, and in the disintegration of post-war Athens it became a hostel for the homeless. In 1952 a zip-manufacturing business took it over. When the company closed down, the property slid into dereliction. It was eventually saved by extensive restoration and re-emerged as the **Athenaeum**, the conservatory of music – set up, predictably, in memory of Maria Callas. Here are practice rooms, a small concert hall where performances range from opera to jazz, a music library and a cool courtyard of verandas and trees.

Almost next door – the last building on Adrianou and facing Thissio station – is another quite elegant building: the restaurant *Vythos*. By day *Vythos* is all peace, apart from the almost choreographed squabbles of the couple who run the fruit stall across the road. Go to *Vythos* to look at the Hephaeston through the trees and to drink *cappuccino freddo*, a drink that except in name is a million miles from its pale, Italian cappuccino sister, or from the ubiquitous *café frappé*. At *Vythos cappuccino freddo* looks more like Guinness: opaque black topped by the whitest froth; a rich bitterness only just balanced by sweetness. From the Athenaeum snatches of music – a phrase of Handel, a faltering trumpeter – seep from the practice rooms, while sesame-biscuit sellers with broad baskets and lottery men with tickets in a cleft stick walk with purpose up the nearly empty street.

To eat here in the evening offers another experience of Athens's frequent collisions of mood and style. At the table outside, excellent fish (the seafood risotto alone is worth a journey), a small but well-thought-out selection of Greek wine, and formal service create one of Athens' more serious restaurants, although its high point is the very traditional *ravani* cake with *kaimaki* ice cream and sour cheery sauce [sic]. No one does it better.

Only twenty metres away every train arriving at Thissio station from the suburbs disgorges ebulliently sociable Athenians set on an evening walk around the *agora*'s cafés; arm-linked chains of young women, families with pushchairs, old men in white shirts ambling in a world that moves at a different speed. Between the restaurant and the station is one of the city's most contested dog territories. Well fed, with fancy collars, the dogs too like to get out at night. Animals in combinations more appropriate to cartoons leap on and off a small raised piece of grass and its containing walls. Small dogs have big-dog patronage, young ones are cuffed into line.

As Adrianou turns left into Apostolou Pavlou there is a little park. Under the trees, students from the Athens School of Fine Arts hold their summer exhibition: this year, a giant porcelain cup and saucer, an Aphrodite stepping tentatively from her shell and a thick, welded iron serpent lying in the grass. Apostolou Pavlou runs left along the south-western edge of the *agora*. Small cafés line Iraklidon and adjacent streets, while another of Athens's delightfully idiosyncratic open-air cinemas, showing both a film and a view of the illuminated Acropolis, is the **Thiseion** at Apostolou 7.

Apostolou Pavlou is a momentous path, leading up to the **Areopagus**, first the criminal court of ancient Athens, later its ruling body, now a small rocky hill to the west of the Acropolis from which it can also be reached (Walk 2). This is the setting for Aeschylus' description of the trial of Orestes for the murder of his mother Clytemnestra, it was where the statesman Demosthenes was tried in 324 BCE and where the notorious and successful courtesan and businesswoman Phryne, who may have been the model for Praxiteles' famous

Wine jug shop on Evripidou

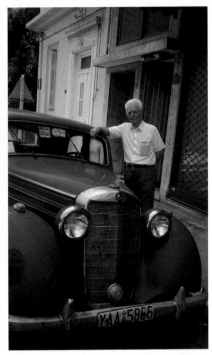

Spoils of war. A 1940s Mercedes

Sunset from the Philopappus Monument

Beach shop, Melanthiou

Central Markets: Athinas

The Old University

Demetrios Rallismansion Panepistimiou   The Tower of the Winds

The Ancient Agora

The National
Library

St George on the Rocks, Anafiotika
Ag. Giorgios tou vrachou

statue, Aphrodite of Knidos, was prosecuted. On trial for murder, her lawyer took the extreme but effective step of stripping her naked to convince the court of her essential qualities. It was a popularly lubricious subject for Victorian painters.

St Paul's visit in 51 CE was to defend virtue of quite another sort (and later gave the street its name). While vigorously addressing a sceptical Council about his faith, he succeeded in converting one of them, Dionysos, who became the patron saint of Athens as St Dionysos the Areopagite.

●

> To the right was Mars Hill, where the Areopagus sat in ancient times, and where St Paul defined his position, and below was the market place where he 'disputed daily' with the gossip-loving Athenians. We climbed the stone steps where St Paul ascended . . . and tried to recollect the Bible account of the matter.
>
> Mark Twain, 1849

●

There are a few scattered remains embedded here – it has yet to be fully excavated – but the most evocative as an idea is a bit disappointing in reality. **The Cave of the Furies**, once a sanctuary for murderers and runaway slaves, is marked by a fall of large stones on the north-east just below the flattened summit with its temple foundations.

The alternative to continuing along Apostolou Pavlou to the left is to walk through trees to the right, which brings you into Eptahalkou which, in turn, swiftly becomes Thessalonikis, a gracious marble-paved street with distinguished neoclassical houses, well restored with particularly attractive architectural details, especially in the friezes and the ornamental scrollwork balconies. Here birds, small gods, swans and flowers are captured in metal fronds. Thessalonikis is also a sad reminder of how many more streets looked in Athens before the crude demolitions of 1950 to 1970.

The small white chapel of **Ag. Athanassios**, on the right, looks more suited to an island than a city congregation. It is an eighteenth-century building on a rock with a much older history. In antiquity it was a sanctuary and tiny cracks in the rock were used to receive offerings. Thessalonikis, now peaceful and dignified, was once a far busier, more dangerous place. Where **Ag. Athanassios** now looks down over the Athens–Piraeus railway line, the sanctuary overlooked the important ancient road from the *agora* to the port and in 86 BCE this was where the harsh Roman general Sulla detected a weak spot in the city defences and breached the city walls before sacking Athens.

Except for the *periptero*, which seems to sell everything imaginable, Athens is a city of single and determined commercial enterprises. Fruit vendors may choose to sell only bananas or only coconuts, myriad small shops sell electric fans, *or* cables, *or* tin jugs, *or* brake pads, *or* honey. Whole streets are dedicated to religious artefacts or to haberdashery. The itinerant binocular-seller sells *only* binoculars, the man who touts CDs never expands into headphones or cheap biros.

At Thessalonikis 7, *To Steki tou Ilia* is a restaurant conceived in this spirit. *Ilia* cooks only – or virtually only – lamb chops, and only in the evening. This evidently fits with the Athenian mindset and the restaurant is one of the most popular in town. After 9.00 p.m. waiters, shining with sweat, rush from table to table and across the road and back, swerving between the huddles of customers waiting for tables. A small boy with a long stick practises his spear-handling with increasingly lethal enthusiasm. Plates of sweet-smelling lamb – small, sinewy-looking chops which can only really be picked up and gnawed – are best consumed with local red wine. Charmingly, *To Steki* has a menu and even at their busiest the waiters go through the motion of taking orders. But unless temptation, in the shape of lamb's entrails, is overwhelming, chops it is.

The affable streets of Thissio come to a dead end at the chaos of a major intersection. Suddenly the Panagi Tsaldari (the Piraeus Road) lies ahead: a vista of uncrossable traffic in every direction, cement stanchions bearing the railway above the road and sheltering a few stranded shops. But there is one splendid and self-important building here, facing outwards to the flyover and the indifferent cars. In 1896, Elias Poulopoulou built himself a small kingdom astride the corner of Iraklidon and Thessalonikis. This is his **Pil-Poul hat factory**. Old prints show a triumphantly busy factory, its chimneys smoking briskly while around it trains and boats take Pil-Poul hats to a fortunate world. In the distance, a mere backcloth to modern enterprise, is old Athens.

The distinctive architecture of the factory has been preserved, as have the delightful blue and yellow ceramic tiles spelling out the name of Poulopoulou. Despite its rather 'solid' new designation, the **Melina Mercouri Cultural Centre** (for a city that owns the mother lode of Western civilization, the affection Athens has for doggedly naming any building vaguely connected with the arts a 'cultural centre' is perplexing) is well worth a visit. The spirit of the original interior has been retained and while the ground floor houses temporary art exhibitions the upper floor recreates, with accuracy and wit, a pre-First World War street. The façades have been constructed from old photographs or salvaged from demolition; the contents are compelling. Here is a barber's, a coffee shop, the gruesome devices and mixtures of a nineteenth-century chemist's, a printer at work in his shirt sleeves. This is an empathetic history of gentility and certainty; of a time when a man might indeed be defined by the ownership of a Pil-Poul hat.

Across the intersection lies **Gazi** (Walk 4): the harder edge of industrialization, and the beginning of the end for a way of life that flowered between 1880 and 1914.

Turn left out of the entrance to the Melina Mercouri Cultural Centre and walk up Iraklidon. There are one or two once-beautiful neoclassical houses in a sad state of decay. They are laments for a nearly irretrievable past. As the road returns towards town there is a proliferation of cafés and several pet shops with ill-tempered but radiantly feathered cockatoos and parrots. This is the more sophisticated side of Thissio and pet-selling has gone up a notch from the songbirds and suspiciously wild-looking rabbits of Adrianou. When Iraklidon meets Apostolou Pavlou turn left and then right to reach the station.

The oldest line in Athens is the **Athens–Piraeus Electric Railway**, ISAP. Taking the train is far and away the most enjoyable way to leave Thissio. Slightly shabby compared to the marble and steel halls of the new Metro, the station, despite being within sight of the Acropolis, has a decidedly suburban feel. A wooden footbridge crosses from the ticket office to the city-bound platform and excited children stand and, through the gaps in the planks, watch the trains pass under them. Birds sing, various unofficial plants straggle down walls and the lines stretch away round a slow bend. It could be some forgotten arm of London's District Line, buddleia and all. Travelling overground in a shallow cutting – the construction of which provided one of the earliest revelations of the extent of the ruins – the track runs along the edge of the *agora*, while on the left-hand side various bits of ancient masonry are left stranded by the course of the railway line. It is a few minutes' journey to Monastiraki or, by changing trains, to the very different worlds of Syntagma or Akropolis.

THE FOURTH WIND
North-West

Skiron

*Carrying embers
from his brazier to
warm the dry winds*

- The Street of Hermes
- The Great and Little Cathedrals
- Ecclesiastical suppliers
- Plato's Academy and the Hill of Colonus
- The ancient cemetery of Keramikos
- The old industrial area of Gazi
- The Technopolis centre of art and technology
- The Hellenic Cosmos museum of virtual history
- Rouf

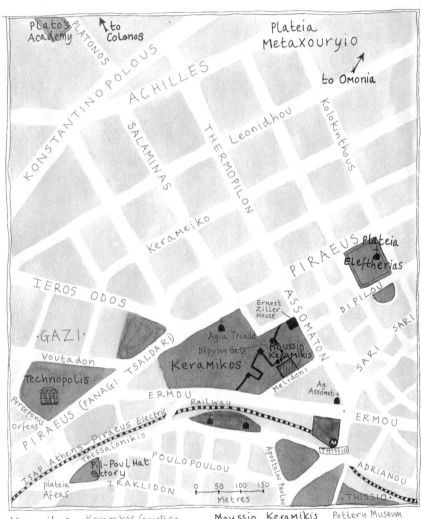

Keramikos   Keramikos Cemetery   Moussio Keramikis   Pottery Museum

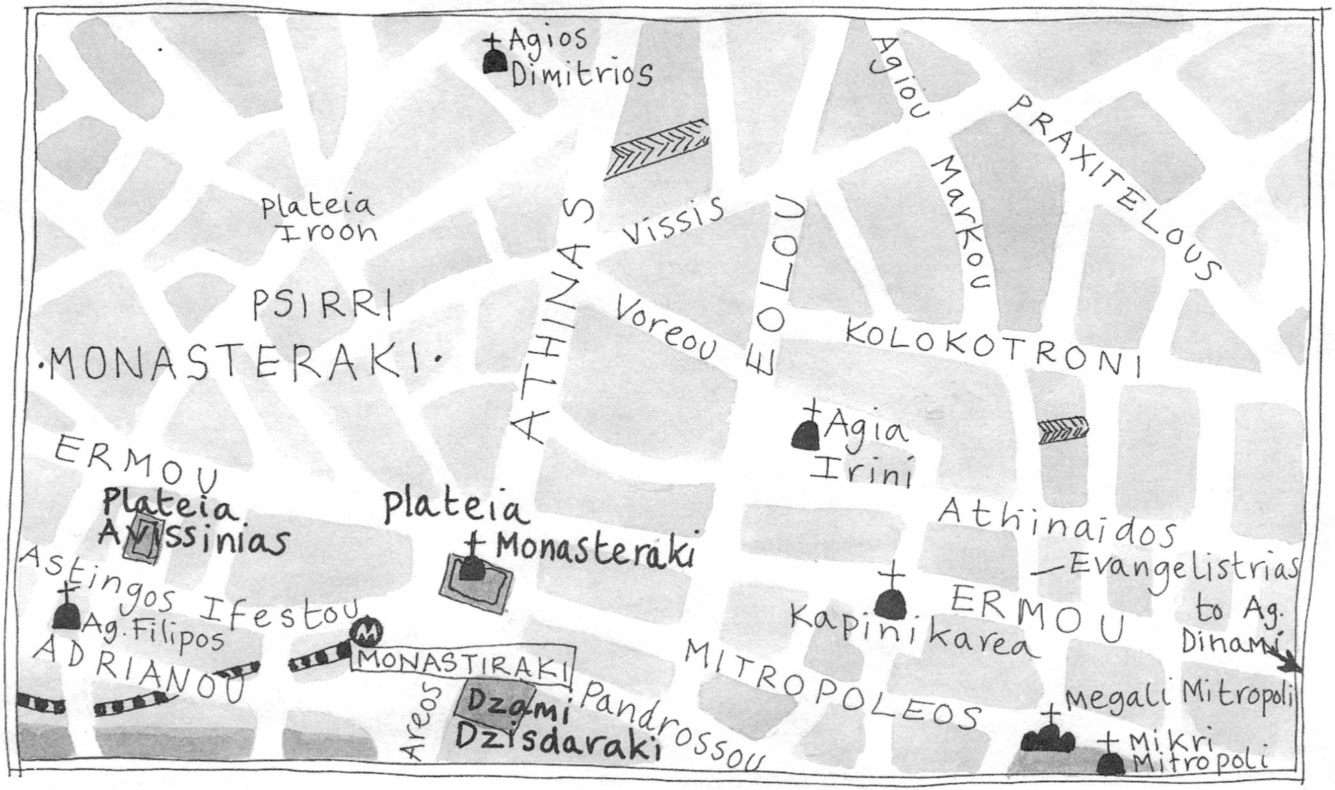

Agios Dimitrios
Plateia Iroon
PSIRRI
·MONASTERAKI·
ATHINAS
Vissis
Voreou
EOLOU
Agiou Markou
PRAXITELOUS
KOLOKOTRONI
Agia Irini
Athinaidos
Evangelistrias
to Ag. Dinami
ERMOU
Plateia Avissinias
Plateia Monasteraki
Monasteraki
Kapinikarea
Astingos
Ifestou
Ag. Filipos
ADRIANOU
MONASTIRAKI
Areos
Dzami Dzisdaraki
Pandrossou
MITROPOLEOS
Megali Mitropoli
Mikri Mitropoli

To travel west across Athens is to follow a straight road. It is, however, not a simple journey, as the route follows a path outwards through concentric circles of history and culture, triumph and devastation. The road is Ermou, named after the god Hermes – the Roman Mercury – a deity who has a firm hold over the imagination of the city and who could not be a more apposite protector and guide.

Hermes races across restaurant signs, advertising and business logos, but above all he lingers over the rooftops of Athens. The edging tiles of neoclassical roofs are one of their most distinctive features. These pretty terracotta carvings, which stand upright and define the roof edge, are called akrokerama, or antefixes; in the evening and the fading light, they are a fretted castellation against the sky. Close to – and their frequent appearance and murky provenance in some antique shops makes examination easy – they encompass a variety of strange and wonderful mythical subjects. There are lotuses and acanthus, there are sirens and images of Athena and occasionally the corner tiles are Janus-like personifications of the wind; there is a handsome one of Boreas (though for how much longer?) on a derelict house in Periandrou in Plaka. But most akrokerama represent Hermes, chubby in a winged helmet, an apparently benign precursor of the Renaissance cherub.

Like so many of the gods, Hermes is a slippery character; an ambivalent friend; a not entirely reassuring presence on the household roof. The ribbons which originally appear plaited around his herald's staff become serpents in later depictions and Hermes has his dark side. He was the eternal child who played exasperating tricks on men and gods, and the ingenious inventor of the lyre and thus all music. In his earliest incarnations he was a phallic god who marked boundaries but in time he became a transcender of them: the divine messenger and patron of all who use the road – merchants, *thieves, traders and travellers. In this role he was also guide to the dead on their journey to the underworld.*

The spirit of this god is never far away as the road leads west from the commercial centre of Athens through its markets to the ancient cemetery of Keramikos, outside the old city walls. The Syntagma Square end is a long stretch of large modern shops – mostly international chains and designer names. By Monastiraki Square, air-conditioned superstores give way to smaller, more idiosyncratic stores, and the outlying stalls and lock-ups of the flea market. From the intersection with Ag. Assomati at Thissio, the wind seems to pick up, blowing dust along the final more exposed stretch of Ermou until it comes to the quiet tombs of Keramikos.

It is worth following Ermou from one end to the other. It is a road that encapsulates the city and its people. Leaving Syntagma and entering Ermou, it is, for a short stretch, a bland, bright street of functional architecture, comparable to any other major shopping centre in Europe. The chain Accessorize punctuates shopping arcades in Greece, and Marks & Spencer, with its insistent radio jingles, is well loved in Athens. (Less loved are Britain's political alliances, and guards in the company's familiarly soothing colours are alert at every door.) Designer boutiques and their chain-store emulators pass in a blast of air-conditioning and music. Young, lacquered shop assistants provide a service that is simultaneously indifferent and intrusive. Touch an item on any shelf and a pair of hands materializes in ritual rearrangement. Muse at a rail and a vigilant assistant stands at your shoulder, ready to nip kleptomanic tendencies in the bud. On payment, an unsmiling checkout girl throws the tautologically termed free gift in the bag. Beware. It is all a matter of goodwill.

Two hundred metres or so after leaving Syntagma Square,

an ecclesiological diversion leads left down Voulis and right into Mitropoleos. This is a glimpse of the power, the mystery, the failings and the endurance of the Greek Orthodox church. On Mitropoleos stands one of Athens's more implacable church survivals: **Ag. Dinami**. The aptly named Chapel of the Divine Power dates from the Ottoman period. Its position is extraordinary: it remains protected in an arcade right under the tall modern ministry of education. It was long the solace of pregnant or infertile women but under later Ottoman rule was briefly a munitions works. Arms smuggled out to the Greeks from here by a worker and a washerwoman were a crucial component in the attack on the Acropolis in the early stages of the War of Independence.

The road continues into the spacious **Plateia Mitropoleos**, a slightly bland, marble-paved square on the northern edge of Plaka, with some pleasant restaurants and cafés. Two hefty statues confront Athens's grandiose and cumbersome cathedral, currently sheathed in its carapace of scaffolding. Built in the late nineteenth century, the **Mitropolis** or Cathedral was constructed from the substance of seventy-two, mostly Byzantine, city churches. Some had been damaged in the War of Independence, others were dilapidated, others simply destroyed to release valuable land. It was not a good beginning.

The Mitropolis is worth seeing, indeed it is unavoidable, but the real gem of this square is the twelfth-century church beside it; already tiny, half hidden behind a handful of orange trees, it is miniaturized by the vast perspective of its neighbour. It is a church of many names for so small a building: **the Mikropolis** or Old Cathedral, the Panayia Gorgoepiköos (the Swift-Hearing Virgin) and, after King Otto was deposed, Ag. Eleftherios (Holy Freedom). It is so tightly tucked into the massive shadow of the cathedral that it appears to be under the newer building's wing. It too is a

Arcade of Ag. Filotheis

bricolage of the past, but a charming one. Built entirely from classical masonry and some remnants of sixth-century churches, it is delightful as a building but also as a fantastical gallery of fragments. In contrast to the predations which succoured the Mitropolis, the Mikropolis was a loving homage to the past built by the twelfth-century Metropolitan of Athens, Michael Choniates. Slices of column, inscriptions, depictions of mythical creatures and dancers are far older than the church itself. Particularly strange and beautiful in its context is the frieze of zodiac signs with illustrations of each month's activities and pagan festivals: a stone Book of Hours. Intermittently crosses have been superimposed to set the hand of the Christian god on these strange symbols.

Pass northwards between the cafés and up **Ag. Filotheis**. At number 17, a solemn old 1930s arcade where the light only just filters through the yellowing glass roof hung with heavy metal lamps, is home to purveyors of sacerdotal goods: tempting as treasure in their dark alcoves. Here are silver-gilt crosses, ornate chalices, censers, matt gold and oil icons, lamps, waxed chests, thick twists of cord and bolts of wonderfully heavily textured brocades, in crimson, green, ivory and purple.

Returning across Plateia Mitropoleos and down Evangelistrias – another street of religious devotion, of the sweet-smelling workshops of icon painters, candle makers,

Athinas

iron-, silver- and goldsmiths – head back to Ermou where Mammon prevails. Almost immediately another small and pretty church stands adamant but dwarfed in size by the mercantile demands of later centuries. The street has to widen to embrace the Byzantine church of **Kapnikarea**, which stands firm in the centre of multi-storey buildings.

Petitioners come and go through Kapnikareas' doors and this is one place where the *laterna* player often lingers. The *laterna* is an old and fading tradition: radio, street music and amplification have overwhelmed it, except as a curiosity. Essentially a barrel organ, the pins are struck by a drum rotated by hand. Experienced practitioners add pins to extend the *laterna*'s range and create their own sounds. It is the prettiest of instruments – a blushing, *fin de siècle* woman is painted as a centrepiece wreathed in flowers, velvet and ribbons and hung about with *komboloi* (worry beads).

As it crosses the top of **Plateia Monastiraki** the well-ordered consumerism of Ermou's early stages crumbles into older, smaller, more haphazard but more essential businesses. To the north, **Athinas** leads to the nineteenth-century food markets, to the south lie the **Aerides**. A third of a kilometre further and it is the workshops, cafés and galleries of Psirri that hide in a tangle of small interconnecting streets to the north and the flea markets of **Plateia Avissinias** to the south.

The sense of Athens as an eastern rather than a western city increases; here the casualties of Middle European upheavals eke out a living. But this is also Athens trading as it always has, no matter that among the goods on sale are car batteries or electric fans as well as tin jugs and china and agricultural tools. From Monastiraki, Ermou is a stretch of workshops or scrap-metal dealers, busy in a haze of engine oil, hot varnish and wood shavings; their windows full of dusty electrical goods or heavy 1930s furniture.

Fan shop, Ermou

Pavements here do not favour the pedestrian. Scooters and motorbikes are parked on any section that does not have fractured and slanting slabs; potholes and abandoned piles of grit or bricks make ambling perilous. Yet it is here that people have time to talk. The bagel sellers and the boys carrying silver trays of coffee from *kafenion* to shopkeeper stop to gossip or read about the football. There are numerous remnants and curiosities of the past in these shabby and apparently simple shops.

At Ermou 100 is a building whose substantial upper storey has arched windows and heavy art-deco pillars. This was once the **local boxing hall**. Mr Karytakis has a small furniture and hardware shop opposite. He used to box in the hall. He was born in 1940 into the worst of the war and his mother insisted that he must learn to fight and when he was seven she sent him up Stadiou to be taught by the famous strongman. The strongman was a hands-on teacher and whirled the little boy around his head and thumped him on the floor three times – Mr Karytakis gives a dangerous demonstration with his *café frappé*. He learned to fight.

Now internationalism is seeping even into this bit of Athens: next door to the old boxing hall is a new Bodum showroom sleek with Scandinavian design, stainless steel and, behind glass that has repelled all dust, a restrained and spotless display of glass coffee jugs and teapots.

At the little intersection with Thissio another Byzantine church, the Ag. Assomati, acts as a roundabout. Its walls are low benches for the weary. On Sundays the Middle Eastern sound of its bells is entirely at one with the flea market. At this point, the **Keramikos** cemetery lies directly ahead. However, for the determined walker or the passionate historian a long detour to the right, setting off up **Odos Ag. Assomaton**, will – eventually – lead to an archaeological site that is little visited despite being freighted with classical

Former Boxing hall, Ermou

associations. **Plato's Academy** is just a wonderfully peaceful, tangled park of ruins in the Athens suburbs.

●

> Besides the leprous-looking coffee houses that have sprung up at the feet of Olympian Jove and are desecrating the place, the peregrinating Greeks make these splendid columns a sort of undressing-room. It is the same with the tomb of Themistocles, the prison of Socrates on the Museum Hill, the excavations in the Keramikos, and every accessible monument a little withdrawn from the public gaze . . . The practice is an heirloom of immemorial antiquity and goes hand in hand, I suppose, with the filth of Martial and the foulness of Athenaeus.
>
> James Albert Harrison, 1878

●

Ag. Assomaton is worth a brief detour, even if the logistical demands of visiting the Academy are too great, just to see on the left the small neoclassical house designed by **Ernest Ziller**, complete with caryatids. It had decided, if inevitably finite, charm in near-dereliction but is newly and beautifully restored. (A copy of it in its original state has been included in the street frontage erected in the old Pil-Poul factory, now a cultural museum (Walk 3).)

To persevere onwards to the Academy, take the road that continues along Thermopilon. There are some attractive residential streets here while others are a little down at heel; it is the epitome of the untroubled and decent Athenian backwater with corner shops and church squares which, silent during the week, are crowded and noisy after mass on Sunday.

After 400 metres in total, two major roads, Achilles and Konstantinopolous, need to be crossed. Bearing slightly right the road ahead is, encouragingly, Platonos. Although it is still a further half-kilometre to the site itself, some battered signs begin to point the way. These die out as you reach the little square of the Academy where the remains stretch off to the left and it is quite easy to walk past assuming that this is simply another overgrown park with a children's playground on its edge.

Before starting to explore, look to the right. At the end of Tripoleos, a street of simple flats, is a small conical hill with a scattering of cypresses. This is a tiny piece of countryside now stranded in a heavily built-up suburb. There are two marked graves on the hill: those of the early nineteenth-century Hellenophiles and scholars Karl Ottfried Muller and Charles Lenormant, who were buried here when this was a quiet grove. A quiet grove of huge significance to lovers of the ancient world. This is **Colonus**, birthplace of Sophocles and the setting for the death of his great protagonist Oedipus.

Chorus: Thou com'st, O stranger, to the noblest
     spot.
Colonus, glistening bright,
Where ever more, in thicket freshly green
The clear-voiced nightingale
Still haunts and pours her song.

Sophocles: *Oedipus at Colonus*

Often I walked the roads round Colonus
Before autumn came, before summer went,
As the sun sank low and the day grew dark,
To tame my wild thoughts and my wild
     thoughts' heart's lament.

No honeysuckle blossomed, no nightingale sang,
No Antigone led blind Oedipus by the hand,
But behind the closed windows where the rebels
     hid
I saw a boy studying the sages' wonderland.

From Nikos Gatsos, 1914–1992:
Evening at Colonos

Plato's Academy is a deceptively large site, a place of random masonry, ravines, grass-covered subsidence and pleasant walks under the trees. Its stone pits are full of rubbish, its thickets blossom with the secrets of courting couples and its glades are havens for puppies and cats. It was partially excavated nearly fifty years ago but in its current state it is a place for the easily inspired romantic rather than the archaeologist, although there are plans to make it more accessible and comprehensible within a bigger archaeological park. As it is, while it may be impossible to make sense of the remains, the imagination can roam unconstrained, particularly as there are rarely any other visitors to the fractured walls and the craters of what was, for 900 years, one of the greatest intellectual centres of the ancient world.

Returning to Thissio, the **Keramikos**, named after the potteries that once dominated the area, spreads out to the north (right) of the road and has its entrance at Ermou 148. It is reasonably easy to catch a taxi to it in the region of the Academy and this avoids retracing the route.

Here, between the chaos of metal workshops and scrap that brings Ermou to its conclusion and the looming gasworks of **Gazi** on Panagi Tsaldari, is Athens's most beautiful archaeological site, marvellously excavated and restored to retain a quiet, timeless seclusion. It was only rediscovered in 1861 when the main road was being laid and its years of interment have protected it well. Among the tangled avenues and grassy terraces of the long-dead are some wonderfully well-preserved monuments, while trees and flowers flourish around a small stream: the marshy remains of the ancient River Eridanous, home to small frogs and terrapins. (It also once provided clay for the potters, just as the dead provided a market for their urns.)

The whole cemetery is a museum to the ancient way of death. Here are decorated sarcophagi, miniature temples, the elaborate tombs of great men, the simple markers of slaves. A selection of stone animals lie on tombs between the trees. They represent vigorous life: an alert dog, a massive bull caught at the moment of its charge. There are urns, stelae and more poignant memorials in stone: a woman saying farewell to her servant and small son, a little girl playing with her puppy, a grandmother with her grandchild on her knee. The epitaph for this last reads: '*I used to hold him of old in those* days, When with living eyes we both looked on the sun; Now that he's dead, I still hold him: for I am dead too.'

Ancient Greeks were always buried outside the city walls and this site was once a great entrance to Athens. The ceremonial way to Eleusis started here and two magnificent gates survive; the **Dipylon Gate** on the road that once led to Plato's Academy but now disappears under the modern city, and the **Sacred Gate**, from which the sacred way set out to Eleusis. Here, too, numerous warriors who once defended their great state are buried and it was here, in 431 BCE, that Pericles gave the funeral oration honouring the dead of the Peloponnesian War.

Mighty indeed are the marks and monuments of our empire which we have left. Future ages will wonder at us, as the present age wonders at us now.

Pericles' Funeral Oration, quoted by Thucydides in the *History of the Peloponnesian War*

Soon this lovely site will be enclosed in a further archaeological park and the trudge down the farther reaches of Ermou, from the living to the dead, with the lorries thundering past towards distant mountains and the sea, will itself be a thing of the past.

The **Sacred Way** (*Ieros Odos*) leads away towards **Rouf** from the Keramikos, but the modern pedestrian must follow Ermou to the point at which it joins the main Piraeus road (Panagi Tsaldari). The skeletons of industrial Gazihori – literally, gas-lands – are huge against the sky; they too are monuments to another age. This was the area of industrial expansion in the nineteenth century and the Gazi factory itself was founded in 1857. It transformed old Athens into new Athens. It brought gas and light and the amenities and aspirations of modern life to the more affluent. To those who lived and worked here, life was hellish; archive photographs show blackened men stoking the furnaces and emaciated children in squalid streets. The miasma of fumes drove out those in neighbouring areas who could escape. This was an area of the poor and the hopeless. Today Gazi is officially upwardly mobile. There are more, strangely eager, claims for it to be known as the Soho of Athens (presumably if Psirri, another nominee, fails some test of artistic seediness). It is a clumsy association; in Gazi, the ambience is as different from Soho's as possible. This area of Athens is much more compelling, more sinister and more raw.

The magnificent **gasometers**, built by Bonnet-Spazin of Lyon in the first years of the twentieth century, have been converted into a superb cultural centre, *Technopolis*, which has retained the weighty grandeur of the industrial machinery and added modern art. It is an exciting experiment, its popularity only curbed at present by the lack of direct transport.

(Much) further down the same road, at 254, in the Tavros district, is another successful industrial conversion, this time of a pre-war factory (Kalithea is the nearest station). The ex-Viosol complex was completed as war broke out and is still an unspoiled modernist design. Taken over by first the Germans, then the Allies, it functioned for a decade or so before its technology became obsolete. It has emerged as an astonishing virtual-reality museum – *The Hellenic Cosmos* – in which it appears that no expense has been spared to create what can only be described as a total experience. It sounds terrible but is in fact rather wonderful. With stereoscopic glasses and a 'magic wand', visitors can step right into the

1904 gasometer, Gazi

Hellenic Cosmos version of Greek history. They see the past and it works.

The complex has the best Internet café in the city, with friendly staff and various other hi-tech exhibitions. For anyone with children, it is probably a godsend.

Most warehouses in Gazi have been converted to clubs and there are a handful of fashionable restaurants. *Mamacas* (**Mummy's Boys**) provides excellent food in slightly self-consciously hip surroundings, yet in the kitchens tradition survives and it is the owners' mothers who cook. *Mamacas* is in Persefonis, which runs parallel to Orfeos; some street planner had an imagination because for all the modern claims, Gazi still has a feel of the underworld – it is only in darkness that it comes alive. By day there is still the shadow of the stale, sweet smell of gas, unforgettable to anyone who has known it. Roads are strings of damp potholes but very few cars come crashing down this way. Although there are plain, well-cared-for houses in bright but fading colours they are interspersed with condemned buildings, low-rent apartments and demolition sites full of old beds, broken glass, convolvulus, wild figs and skinny cats. Angry graffiti explodes over Gazi's walls and torn strips of black fabric hang as pennants from shabby flats, from workshops, from private houses. Here the messages are not translated into English but they are nonetheless clear.

At Voutadon, which passes down the side of Technopolis, a bright yellow café sits in a small garden, oblivious under the metal spars and lattices of the gasometers. *I Eftihia Sto Gazi* translates as 'Happiness in Gazi' and, sitting here with an ouzo, Gazi's strange appeal slowly draws one in. Walk down Voutadon and you reach a long railway line stretching between an avenue of thin trees into the city in one direction, to the mountains in the other. Except when a train passes with a long blast of its horn, it is a silent place; a few men sitting at tables, a few women crossing the lines with bags of shopping to characterless blocks of flats on the far side. Then turn back towards the city; from Gazi there is really nowhere else to go.

Return late at night and the edginess and the pools of darkness between buildings blank by day but now pulsing with green and red lights, and the fast beat of music behind guarded doors reinvent Gazi. At Voutadon 34 the radical theatre group *Schedia* puts on Berthold Brecht, Pirandello and improvised plays about alienation and parricide; angry and radical themes that Euripides might still recognize. On Panagi Tsaldari the deliberately seedy yet exotic nightclub *Tessera*, with its striptease, its gay evenings and its cult following, is currently fashionable.

Another strangely disorientating experience awaits those willing to walk to **Rouf station**, up Ieras Odos (north-west of

Keramikos, on the city side of Technopolis). *To Treno sto Rouf* is Athens's most unusual and distinctive restaurant and theatre. A 1947 steam engine with seven carriages has been restored to provide a stage, bar and dining room. Cocktails, varnished wood, subtle lighting and the sound of distant trains pulling in and out of the station create a pleasantly unsettling atmosphere. (Bookings can be made at Makrigiani 5–7, near Akropolis station.)

It is usually possible to park around Gazi, but the alternative is a return walk down a quite relentless stretch of road to the metro at Thissio. By night this is a feasible journey, though one best completed briskly. By day, although the furnaces and smokestacks have long since cooled, Skiron's embers still heat the gusts of wind and the traveller's steps falter as they turn back from the cemetery and the trains and the strippers and the gas, towards life and the city.

THE FIFTH WIND
North

Boreas

Who sounds a conch shell, his cloak in heavy folds blown by the coldest winter winds

- Oriental Monastiraki
- The Tzisdarakis mosque
- Athinas
- The Central Markets
- The merchants of Evripidou
- The cafés, bars and galleries of Psirri
- Plateia Avissinias and the flea market
- The tourist shops of Pandrossou

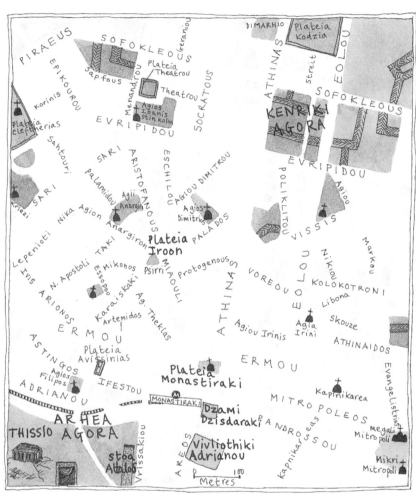

Megali Mitropoli   Cathedral
Mikri Mitropoli   Old Cathedral
Dimarhio   Town Hall
Arhea Agora   Ancient Agora

Kendriki Agora   Central Market
Vivliothiki Adrianou   Hadrian's Library
Thissio   Temple of Hephaestus
Dzami Dzisdaraki   Tzisdarakis Mosque

Even in summer, daylight often feels far away from Monastiraki; it is a region of the enclosed. Arcades shaded by whorls of iron foliage and old lamps shelter cavernous junk shops, basement booksellers and old cafés. Small dark churches lit only by their sanctuary lamps, and vaulted food markets, create a mood unique to this area. Then there are the narrow streets of cramped shops, full of spices, tallow and twine or tubs of olives or pulses; even where the alleys are open to the sky they are so often made narrow by the trays and rails of wares or the parked trucks full of flowers that daylight seems far away.

Buildings of every age and function hang on, hidden behind shops or more modern exteriors; decaying or converted fragments of beauty and exoticism. The vestiges of Ottoman culture that once dominated the city but that have in most places been obliterated still exist here, both in buildings and in the mood of the streets.

In the streets around Omonia and Plateia Monastiraki the diverse strands that make up modern Athens are more instantly apparent. Here it is all about vigorous survival: of men and women, of history, hope, houses, cultures, economies, even dogs and cats. Small businesses, markets and craftsmen, itinerant traders and beggars ply their trade.

Only comparatively recently have Africans and Asians begun to live in Athens, and their numbers remain small. More noticeable are the refugees and migrants from the troubled Balkans; Albanians in particular have a hard time of it here.

The dark-eyed children who descend on restaurants, tentative in young childhood, worryingly adept by ten or so, are a fact of Athens life. Even their reasonable cleanliness and adequate clothing is deliberate: when the organized trafficking of children first began – for this is what you see – they were in rags but overt suffering proved to be not as commercially productive as cuteness. That their attempts to sell unwanted goods or play a mouth organ are so inadequate, or their routine of physical affection so clumsy, only makes them more pathetic. The future of the skinny eight-year-old child who smiles and sulks and tosses her black hair is hardly in doubt.

The children hover, waiting for preoccupied authority. When they are rounded up by agile waiters, some leave with heads low, unsold flowers trailing in the dust. Others laughingly dodge their pursuers, taunting them from across tables.

At one 'superior' restaurant a duo of real ability is tolerated by the staff. A girl of perhaps twelve or thirteen, her long hair caught up in a ponytail, her small body stiff and upright, holding herself like a dancer but with a wary face, has a voice uncannily more mature than her years. Her rendition of 'Ave Maria' stops all talk at the tables. A jovial man in his forties accompanies her on a violin. The audience is enthusiastic, money is handed over, he takes it, the girl is admired, patted. Throughout the performance she looks away.

●

The Monastiraki station was packed; it was the closing-time rush hour, closing time for offices, folk art and souvenir shops, furniture shops and smart boutiques on Ermou Street nearby; a motley crowd converged on the station. She grew desperate; they could easily miss each other in the rush. She sat down on a bench near the left-hand exit, so as to be facing the first carriage when the train came in. She let her gaze wander beyond the precincts of the station. She noticed some of the old buildings still surviving in Athens; old walls corroded by humidity, wrought-iron balconies with griffins or swans, broken ornamental roof tiles. From a distance they looked pretty, but she couldn't help feeling glad that her own two-storey house, built soon after the war, stood in green, peaceful isolation in Kifissia.

Menis Koumandareas: *Koula* (1991)

Monastiraki is best explored beginning at its metro station. On **Plateia Monastiraki**, immediately opposite the exit, is the **Tzisdarakis mosque**, dating from 1750, now minus its minaret which was destroyed, as a symbol of all that was loathed about the Ottoman occupation, at the start of the War of Independence. (The mosque is now a **Museum of Ceramics**.) Close by is the church which was once the monastery that gave the whole area its name. Until 1820 the monastery stretched beyond the city walls but its buildings were destroyed for archaeological excavations and further depredations came about in the building of the railway.

Behind the church, under a length of glass-roofed arcade, supported on the wonderful metal fronds and curls, lamps rusting slightly, is *Bairaktaris*, founded in 1879 and thriving on tradition: tripe soup, long-dead celebrities and the blessing of the Greek Orthodox church. *Bairaktaris* already owns the stretch of tables and high-ceilinged restaurants along its side of the square and has ambitions to cross the road and spread on inexorably. The logistics of Athenian restaurants are a challenge. Kitchens to one side of a square serve tables across two lanes of unforgiving traffic, or stuck in a park, or up three flights of steps.

At *Bairaktaris* they have co-opted modern technology so that when the time comes to pay, the energetic waiter has to galvanize the creatively sulky girl who does the bills by ringing her on his mobile. Inside, ceiling-high mirrors, the

Tzisdarakis mosque

usual black-and-white shots of 1960s politicians and film stars, a large crucifix and various little saints form a background to a trio on electric bouzouki, guitar and accordion.

Outside is a lot more of the same. Music is a territorial business. The trios know their limits; it sometimes seems that all Athens is carved up between the musicians: the little boys exhaling tunelessly through mouth organs, the itinerant trumpeters, the *laterna* players and the occasional Eastern European fiddlers. The effect on those caught on the auditory boundary is extraordinary: the *Bairaktaris* musicians do traditional music, emotional laments and jolly island folk songs; the others are not narrowly nationalist – if it is syrupy they can play it, from 'O Sole Mio' to 'The Last Rose of Summer' and always, always, as if in some terrible compact with the tourists, 'Never on Sunday' and 'Zorba's Dance'.

A roving Romany band roves just as far as the corner, while a second trio (or third, if you count *Bairaktaris*'s own, smug indoors) moves in from the side. This bouzouki player knows his stuff (although the stuff he knows is all too familiar after half an hour) but his instrument is a thing of great and antique beauty. The accordion player has dignity and strong arms, but the guitar player has evidently been co-opted just to keep the trio up to the required number. He strums, randomly and glumly, out of tune, out of rhythm and permanently out of countenance, on three strings.

Wandering salesmen pass by in affable if half-hearted attempts to shift their goods. It is hard to imagine where lies the demand for Russian watches, or the two-metre fans and teak giraffes sold by young West Africans, or the fairy lights, posters of mustachioed War of Independence heroes, or whistles that sound like songbirds. (The latter unintentionally ironic, given the menu in these parts.)

Almost due north, up **Athinas**, are the great covered food markets of Athens, the **Kentriki Agora**. At their core are fish and meat markets feeding the city as they have for two thousand years, but doing so now in great halls built in the nineteenth century. They are coming under pressure, largely from the EU, to change their ways, to pay more than lip service to sanitation, electric fly-killers, health inspectors. The goddess Hygeia may yet be invoked to bring down the food markets. Today the noise, the smell, the lights and the gleaming piles of produce are wonderful and shocking; they assault all the senses at once – an Aladdin's cave of flesh.

In the fish hall it is a shimmering scene: the iridescent silvers, pinks, petrol blue and graphite of every conceivable seafood; craggy or nacreous shells, bound pincers and glutinous whelks stranded on great floes of ice. In the meat hall porphyry liver, piglets hanging from racks, great sides of beef or lamb, creamy offal and the bronze feathers of game birds are piled up in aisle after aisle.

The fishmongers and the butchers are a display in themselves, enticing or demanding attention, shouting down the quality of their neighbours' goods. Strong, loud and unflinching, they confront the Athenian housewife, the choosy restaurateur and the old man just wanting sprats for his dinner with equal vigour.

The **fruit and vegetable market** is to the side; here the smell is of orchards and the vivid colours are less disturbing than in the carnivores' emporia. Every conceivable fruit is sold and the staples from the maize of old to the much more modern but now essential tomato: scarred, misshapen, plump, sweet and perfect. There are marvellously shaped varieties of musty fungus, greys and cream, gilled and fluted. In each section the mood is different; greengrocers are milder, more diffident merchants than the hard men of the meat hall or the wits trading fish.

In adjacent *stoa* and lanes are cheese ghettos, ranging from crumbling *feta* to the ochre brown of provincial hard cheese and tiny nuggets in dark liquor. There are preserved-fruit stalls in the street: sticky dates, sugar-dusted figs, bananas withered into sweetness, currants and raisins, and tiny stores turned into fortresses by the hemp sacks of pulses and beans along the pavement outside.

I give the name 'rose-dish' to this casserole; it is prepared in such a fashion that when you get it you may not have merely a sauce fit to wreathe the head, but even inside of you, you may feast your little body with a complete dinner. I crushed the most fragrant roses in a mortar, then laid on carefully boiled brains of fowls and pigs, from which the stringy fibres had been removed, also the yolks of eggs; then olive-oil, garum-sauce, pepper and wine. All this I stirred thoroughly and placed in a new casserole, giving it a fire that was gentle and steady.

Athenaeus: *The Deipnosophists* (second century BCE)

●

Turn back down Athinas and wander either way down **Evripidou** and the little streets off it. It is impossible to do *more* than wander: the narrow pavements are rough and congested with buyers, traders, boxes, bikes, precarious displays and oblivious passers of the time of day. Here are spice and tea shops where dried oregano appears next to saffron – rarely used in Greece, although grown in some quantity – and rosemary, used in incense but not on lamb (smacking too much of sacrifice). And joss sticks.

Shops on Evripidou

The spice merchants are intellectuals, travellers, men once of the world who have retreated. At number 45 is traditional charcuterie: sausages, salamis, *pastourama*, made the same way in the same place since the 1920s. At *Elixir*, Evripidou 41, a bearded Greek, handsome and huge, sits under a ceiling heavy with long stalactites of unidentifiable dried things, in a shop smelling of camomile and full of waxed-paper packets, candles, jars of honey and tiny drawers of mystery. He carefully weighs and makes up individual combinations of tea for customers. The dried goods tend to spread out down Evripidou and the flower stalls are traditionally down Eolou, which runs parallel with Athinas to the east, and group around **Ag. Irini**.

Streit has the best of honey shops, decorated, unsurprisingly but prettily, with bees. Honey in the morning (soap to wash with), honey in the evening (a candle to light the way), honey at suppertime (sweet pastries), honey from day to night in furniture wax or as a health supplement. The versatility of the Greek bee is a wonder.

Westward down Evripidou are the household goods. The ubiquitous spoutless wine-jugs in turquoise, gold and red metal, and rack after rack of tin utensils (spouts and letter boxes could be an entrepreneurial opportunity in Athens). String, rope, flex, chain: everything is tied up, tied down or tied together in Athens. Trade is, strangely, most hectic and most argumentative at the cork shop. Next door an elderly window display sells dusty hardware seduction. A red-checked tablecloth, knives and forks laid for two, plastic goblets filled with red liquid, a plastic lobster and plastic flowers and, just to show this is a classy fantasy, a no-smoking sign.

It is always difficult to cross the space in the centre of town, at the branching off of the streets of Aeolus and Hermes. It is there that the citizens, sitting before the coffee houses or standing in the middle of the street, discuss the questions of peace and war.

Edmond About, 1852

Around the central market there are numerous, almost nameless, tiny **ouzeris** where hungry traders and customers can eat the best of the food available all around them. These are robust local dishes. Tripe broth and pigs' trotters are basics but there are less challenging alternatives for those who want to eat very late and very well. One of the best, particularly in winter, but hardest to identify is *Diporto*, in a basement with no sign but encouraging aromas, at Theatrou 1.

On the corner with Socrates, above the market in the **Stoa Athenaton**, is one of Athens's most authentic **rebetika** clubs. Only open between 11 p.m. and early morning, when the markets start up again, *Rebetika Istoria* is crowded, smoky and so Greek that an outsider can only really look on. It is a glimpse of an Athenian past that was often desperate and impoverished rather than glamorous or romantic.

Rebetika grew out of a fusion of the eastern music brought with the refugees from Turkey, and particularly Smyrna (Izmir), in the forced repatriations of 1923. Greek by blood but often assimilated in Turkey, the immigrants found themselves largely unwelcome in Athens. Out of the blending of their musical traditions with those of the poorest city dwellers already there, from lives lived on the edge of criminality and destitution came the blues of *rebetika*. Since this music was originally fuelled by hashish, oppression and suffering, there are those who argue that relative affluence and stability will turn *rebetika* into a historical curiosity. Perhaps it is already on the downside of its revival, having become almost mainstream – or as mainstream as a genre created from despair, violence, drugs and death can be.

Rebetika

Play the bouzoukis, play, lads,
Because a suffering soul is asking you.
Play tonight, so that a poor bum's
Heart can break.

I gambled my life with you,
I paid for the damage you did
With blood.
Anything I ever had,
I lost it in one night
Because I placed my trust
In your black soul.

You've left two hearts in mourning.
My poor mother is suffering too,
She who brought me up with so
Much night-time suffering,
So that your two black hands
Could strangle me.

V. Tsitsanis

For the daytime visitor to Athinas and Evripidou there is one oasis in the density of people, smells, noise and sights. Off the western end of Evripidou shortly after it crosses Athinas, turn left down Ag. Dimitrios and then left again into Melanthiou. This **small square at the back of Ag. Dimitrios church** is as brightly coloured as the markets, but only occasional pedestrians enter it. The precincts of the church provide an opportunity to sit in the shade but it is also an almost museum-standard display of the joy of plastic. On one side is a jolly shop selling Lilos, beach balls, deckchairs, buckets, spades and huge inflatable lobsters. The smell of childhood, of paddling pools and cycle repair kits, is evocative and warm on the breeze; but the explosion of colour along the right-hand side is in a sensory league of its own.

Here is a tropical grotto of flowers spreading like the worst nightmare of genetic engineering into the depths of the shop, up to the first storey and across the street: familiar shades, familiar flowers, but rarely the two in natural conjunction; these are mutant varieties of size and growth. The street is dense with weeping fuchsias, mats of vines, fluorescent rose trees, strings and swathes of bougainvillea in indigo and gold, exuberant morning glory shrubs in pots. Hefty water lilies, white, tinged with vermilion, nestle next to monster mushrooms, and the odd crab lingers in a basket filled with aubergines and carrots. This too is a shrine to the plastic art.

It is all gloriously false, from leaf to stamen to fin. Old ladies, black with widowhood, bent with age and fresh from the consolations of Ag. Dimitrios, stop in surprise. Again and again hands reach out, uncertainly, to touch or smell.

From the outside Ag. Dimitrios itself is unpromising: bulky, covered with rough cement and (long) awaiting restoration. Around it a marble courtyard is invariably wet and lethal. No warning notice here: the caretaker beams, makes a redundant tumbling motion with his mop and invokes the saint's assistance for all falling visitors. He is very keen on visitors. 'Good. Good,' he says, pointing at the open door.

The interior of the church is dark with varnish and candle smoke. The iconostasis is magnificently impregnable, the Virgin Mary flakes and fades into nothing in a frieze of painted saints while a constellation of stars shine against a midnight apse. Weighty chandelier fall almost to head height; the light reflected by dull gold pigment and silver-framed icons is subsumed by darkness. The mystery survives the cleaner moving down the aisles and timing the movements of her broom to her conversation with an invisible interlocutor somewhere outside. The caretaker's dog slinks in; a small 1950s drawing-room clock – a gift from a benefactor – chimes electronically.

The caretaker himself is all proprietorial pride. This church is a family business; outside two metal tables form a café run by 'my good friend'. A large youth, hands and spirit deep in his pockets, moves slowly and unsmilingly across the road while an older man shouts at his back. 'My nephew is good boy,' the caretaker says half-heartedly.

Turn left outside Ag. Dimtrios and into Aeschylus and after a hundred metres or so you arrive at the grandly named but small and unremarkable **Plateia Iroon**: the Square of the Heroes. The heroes are those of the War of Independence who met here to plan their ultimately successful insurrection. The lottery of Greek street-naming means that the whole range of great Greeks of the past may find themselves, like Asclepius or Byron or Democrates, the eponymous heroes of insignificant alleys or scruffy arcades. Aeschylus and Euripides were surely intended for the road to one of Athens's 123 theatres and Hippocrates for one leading to a hospital. The poet Pindar leads through greenery to the lyrical Lycabettus Hill but Sophocles is home to the **Athens Stock Exchange** and the Street of the Evzones passes quietly through parks and past hospitals, a church and a museum of music before terminating more appropriately behind the heavily fortified US Embassy.

Avenues named after members of the Greek royal family have come and gone and come again as views of the monarchy shift from enthusiasm to hostility to indifference and many tourists have cursed Greek intransigence on finding, eventually, that Eleftherios Venizelou is always called Panepistimiou – except on the map.

So Plateia Iroon is in itself unheroic: a reassuringly workaday place with a paper shop, a barber, some café tables and benches. It is perhaps what the heroes fought for. The little streets that lead off it are home to the soaring upward mobility of the neighbourhood of **Psirri**, which has few grand buildings but is a place of great appeal by day and a quite different sort of charm and vigour by night. It is an area bounded by Athinas, Ermou and the Piraeus road, and dense with small businesses and workshops.

It is also second only to Plaka in having some of the city's most appealing small churches, invariably set in their own peaceful courtyards; there is even a chapel under the **old criminal courts** in Kakourgiodokiou 4, and at Kriezi 10 is the **Armenian Church of Athens** with its onion dome. On the corner of Evripidou and Menandrou, **Ag. Ioanis stin Kolona** was erected around a Roman column that survives, still displaying its Corinthian capital and still believed to have the power to cure fever.

In the nineteenth century **Psirri** was a notoriously criminal environment: a no-go area run by a long-haired armed Greek mafia known as *koutsavakides* who, dressed in their intimidating uniform of fedora and black jacket, extorted money from government officials and small businesses. One more modern local hero was D. Bairaktaris, head of the Athens police in the late nineteenth century, who went in to Psirri in person, armed with a bullwhip and accompanied by some haircutters, to disarm and disperse the gangs.

Originally a working-class area, a region of blacksmiths, and home to many exiles from the islands of Naxos and Karpathos, Psirri has retained the element of craftsmanship even as it has become more fashionable (it is the other contender for the inexplicably desirable 'Soho of Athens' title). Its prettier houses have been restored, its warehouses turned into galleries. There are still music workshops, lacemakers, box-makers, copper- and bronze-beaters, chandlers, icon painters, cobblers, tobacconists, carpet traders and leather-workers going about their business and through doors and windows men can be seen quite alone, and utterly preoccupied, restoring a chair or a guitar, repairing a toaster or motorbike motor. The defining noise of Psirri by day is hammering and sanding.

By night the sound changes register, to music and loud conversation as crowds fill the streets between numerous small eating places, from tapas bars to tavernas, wine bars, traditional coffee houses, pastry shops, sushi bars, Indian food and Italian restaurants. Among the best is the seafood at *Taverna tou Psirri* at Aeschylou 12, run by an islander who knows his fish and his cheese, and also at *Naxos* and at *Psipsina*, a frosted white and silver fantasia with vivid modern paintings. *Bee* and *Guru* are currently the favoured bars for music. *Bee*, true to its name, sells honey by day. At *Enastron* good food is served in a fine conversion of a neoclassical house, in the street named Mikonos, after Mikon, an ancient coppersmith and sculptor whose skills and inclinations would still fit in well in Psirri. He was thought to be the lover of Aspasia, wife of the uncompromising Pericles, and it was here that they were believed to meet in secret.

There is another famous lover and hero beloved by Greeks who has links to Psirri. **Lord Byron** (Walk 1) lodged in this area in 1809 on his first visit to the city and it was there, at Thekla 11, that he developed a passion for Teresa Makri, his landlady's daughter, a passion immortalized in his poem 'The Fair Maid of Athens'. It was not one of his greatest works. Makri was just twelve years old at the time. When Byron returned to Athens two years later Teresa's mother pressed him on the subject of marriage to her daughter. He confided to his friends that he was vastly amused. A quarter of a century later the muse lived in a hovel with her numerous children, her beauty long faded. She died in poverty.

By those tresses unconfined,
Wooed by each Aegean wind;
By those lids whose jetty fringe
Kiss thy soft cheeks' blooming tinge;
By those wild eyes like the roe,
Zoë mou sas agapo.

By that lip I long to taste;
By that zone-encircled waist;
By all the token-flowers that tell
What words can never speak so well;
By love's alternate joy and woe,
Zoë mou sas agapo.

Maid of Athens! I am gone:
Think of me, sweet! when alone.
Though I fly to Istambol,
Athens holds my heart and soul:
Can I cease to love thee? No!
Zoë mou sas agapo.

George Noel Gordon, Lord Byron
(1788–1824)

Psirri is not just about mending, eating, worshipping or making love. There are eight **theatres** in this small area: the *Ivi* (satire), *Thesion* (avant-garde to Shakespeare) and *Apotheke* are the best known and one of Athens's smarter open-air cinemas is *Lipton Ice* at Sari 40–44. But it is **art galleries** that have precipitated Psirri's gentrification.

Epistrofi occupies two eye-catching houses at Taki 5–8, but new galleries and their aficionados arrive every month.

Heading broadly south, you reach the end of Psirri at Ermou. Crossing over from Karaisaki or Artemidos you come into **Plateia Avissinias**, the hub of the famous **Monastiraki flea market**. No doubt there are prizes to be found among the accumulation of junk; irresistible fragments of unknown lives. From antiques to religious kitsch, from collector's items to tourist souvenirs of the most deliciously awful kind to fallen-off-the-back-of-a-lorry booty, still-packaged electrical goods, there is not a lot that can't be bought in Avissinias and its surrounding streets.

On Sunday the permanent market explodes over the whole area. Bargains, monstrosities and rags are draped over the hoardings of excavations, dumped in pathetic piles of fabric and magazines, all slipping one into another along the road edge like some overblown and fading herbaceous border.

Chair shop

The medical-instruments stall outside *Café Avyssinia* is not for the faint-hearted. There is suspicious rust on the chest-openers, needles still project from wartime syringes and blue and green glass stoppered bottles have murky sediments. Around the corner a large lock-up is selling everything necessary to equip an army. Camouflage nets, bandoliers, flying suits, grenades and military radio sets. Possibly the fact that all Greek men still do national service brings some of this warware onto the market; it is a pretty impressive collection. The suitably combative-looking stall keeper sits in a deckchair with a minute kitten wrapped in a blue shawl blissfully supine in his lap. He whispers endearments to it while stroking its stomach. His grizzled friend looks on in admiration. This is a man.

Café Avyssinia to one side of the square is a perfect place to stop and watch it all. The menu is in Greek – order at random, for any surprise will be a good one – or ask the young owner who speaks excellent English. The Piaf-like laments of Alkestis Protopsalti (a singer long overdue for recognition outside Greece) alternate with Cuban mixes in its cool and faintly art-deco interior; wonderful Macedonian food is served: fresh sardines in vine leaves, baked spicy cheese and tabouleh.

Then, dodging between the barrows and stalls of the Plateia, turn left out of Avissinias into **Ifestou**. This is a bazaar of cheap clothing, football strip, resin busts of Athenas and an understandably worried-looking Plato. Crossing Plateia Monastiraki, the flea market continues up **Pandrossou**, a street of exuberant display.

It is dark again in narrow Pandrossou as T-shirts and cheesecloth hang like regimental colours from racks above the shops. There are Barbie gods and goddesses here, a brilliant marketing idea: Athena, Poseidon, Hercules in a plastic lion-skin shell, Aphrodite in pink and big hair – Barbie was made for reincarnation as the goddess of love – and Hermes, nifty in a rayon chiton and long legs. All the gods wear fishnet pants. There is a carousel Parnassus like a huge iced cake, rotating slowly, lit from the inside and with all the gods standing to attention.

But mostly there is shop after shop of Greek blue *I love Athens* mugs, Parthenon snowstorms, and T-shirts, sometimes with the words of Kazantzakis or Homer but more often with a peculiarly Greek wit that fails to translate: 'Sperminator. I will return,' says a cartoon condom, 'Me I am also not feeling too good' laments a citric-green vest. Even in Roman times, tourists complained about souvenirs – the cost, the taste. Nothing is new in Athens.

But there are also **second-hand bookshops**, selling 1960s film fanzines and lurid posters for Greek gangster movies, Marxism yesterday or boxing matches, and boxes and boxes of books. At Ifestou 24, a small arcade leads to a basement bunker lit by solitary bulbs and with books stacked from floor to ceiling. At the far end the delightful **Georgiou Achille** holds court in his tiny shop surrounded, inside and out, by precariously balanced piles of artefacts that fill a category somewhere between junk and antiques. He talks the talk, somewhat undercut by his friends who wait happily for the performance, prompting him from time to time. He sells *akrokerama* and Turkish brass coffee pots but his speciality is votive objects – the small thin silver plaques that direct divine concentration on an area of affliction. There are limbs, eyes and large ears and, inevitably, infants. There are men in hats and women in aprons. There must also have been those who wanted God's mechanical intercession with an ailing car, or so it seems from the occasional 1950s Cadillac. Ancient Greeks might be puzzled by the cars but the rest they would recognize very well.

Between the endearing rubbish and the house clearances, there are a handful of more serious shops. Melissinos is a poet and sandal-maker. In his eighties now, he still sits and sews, with a certain self-awareness, in his simple shop at Pandrossou 89. There are tens of different sandal styles, some little changed from when human beings first shod themselves. 'Am I like Hermes, dad?' asks a chubby little Asian-American boy with glasses, lacing up his transforming thongs.

Arcade in Monastiraki flea market

While contemplating the sandals, customers are made aware that Melissinos's literary works are also available, as are testimonials from wearers (The! Beatles! Cary Cooper) and readers. There are formal letters from the Universities of Cambridge, Oxford and Harvard, a slightly equivocal response from the editor of the *Princeton Encyclopaedia of Poetry and Poetics* ('Some of the stanzas are very memorable. I shall reread them from time to time'), a plethora of newspaper cuttings from Germany, France and Britain. The poetry is good but for a more unusual pleasure read Melissinos's dramatized version of *Lady Chatterley's Lover*, which although in an English translation has acquired a decidedly Mediterranean level of unrepressed emotion.

Further up Pandrossou, at number 50, a long-term occupant of the corner site, is the antique shop *Martinos*, a restrained, classy emporium of serious antiques since before

The Two Cathedrals

Roman columns outside Ag. Ekaterini

Theatre of Herodes Atticus and Hill of the Muses

Pil-Poul hat factory

Ziller house in Ag. Asomaton

Temple of Hephaestus

Traditional shadow puppets

The National Gardens

Bird shop in Thissio

Graffiti in Exarchia

the Second World war. Dowry chests, candlesticks: a few good pieces, displayed in dignity. At night, when Pandrossou is an empty, silent alley, its shops boarded or covered in grilles, a solitary trumpeter sometimes plays on this corner and his notes echo hauntingly all the way back to Monastiraki. Ahead lies Greek Orthodoxy: the square of the **Great and Little Cathedrals**. Behind, back down Pandrossou, lies the strange and ephemeral mixture of pragmatism and trade, charm and squalor that, as much as any ruin, connects Athens with its many pasts.

THE SIXTH WIND
North-East

Kaikias

*Dressed in a mantle,
he carries a shield
of hailstones*

- The neoclassical mansions of Panepistimiou
- The Academy
- The commercial centre of Omonia
- Exarchia and the bookshops of the university quarter
- The National Archaeological Museum
- The Museum of Theatre
- Kolonaki
- The Gennadion Library
- The funicular
- Lykavittos

🏠 Academy, University, National Library

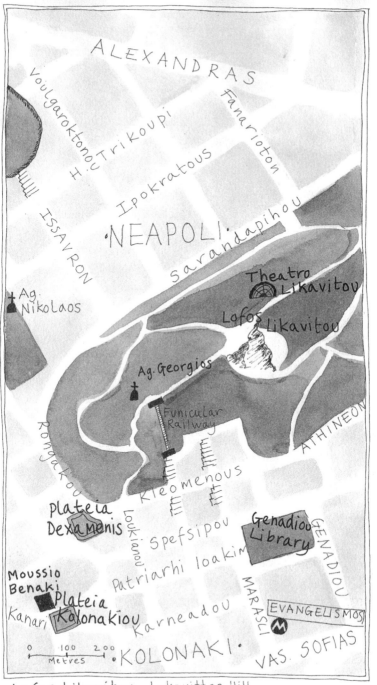

Lofos Likavitou Lykavittos Hill

Syntagma is the starting point, yet again, this time for a walk through the imposing intellectual and financial centre of Athens. A street with two names: the wide thoroughfare officially known as Eleftherios Venizelou is invariably – and to the confusion of visitors – called Panepistimiou, and leads north-west from the square along the side of the Hotel Grande Bretagne.

Panepistimiou runs from residually elegant Syntagma to brasher, more commercial Omonia. Neither centre is quite what it believes itself to be. Progress has diluted Syntagma's patrician air just as it has cleaned up the sleaze and buzz of Omonia. Panepistimiou, though, still lives up to the aspirations of those who laid it out and designed its triumphant if sometimes overwhelming public buildings.

There are few ancient sites to see in this area but the inspiration and legacy of the classical world is radiantly reflected in some of the finest neoclassical architecture in the world. Panepistimiou is the one street in Athens where neoclassicism flowered in the nineteenth century and remained in bloom.

But this distinctive and much-admired style of building is not, as it might appear, the direct descendant of the grandest buildings of antiquity. Byzantine buildings were Greece's natural heritage and classicism returned to Greece largely through an accident of timing. French and English romanticism had been kindled by the experiences of the Grand Tour and fuelled by the finds coming out of Italian archaeological sites like Pompeii and Herculaneum. When the Greeks won independence from Turkey they were ready (indeed eager) to embrace European ideas of superior beauty, driven not least by the wish to replace the oriental style that represented the hated occupation.

Classicism was, obviously, made for the Greeks. And if they were to embrace it, then battered, semi-deserted, isolated Athens would be the natural choice as its capital. Nafplion in the Peloponnese had already been established as the seat of the monarchy and de facto capital, but it was Athens that possessed the vital spirit and physical fragments of the great Hellenic ideal. This mood of paradoxically forward-looking retrospection would embrace not just the way ruins were retrieved and restored but the design of the new city.

At independence there were no architects living in Athens. The young architects who flooded into Athens were to change the face of the city. Mostly Germans and Danes, they included Schubert, Hansen, Ziller and the Frenchman, Boulanger. Any attempt at integrating Byzantine with classical forms tended to come from Greeks such as the Bucharest-educated Kleanthis and the brilliant Kaftanzoglou.

Relationships between architects were not as disciplined or harmonious as their creations. They engaged in bitter fights to wrest the best commissions from each other, even to take over projects already halfway to completion.

Yet although grandiose classical schemes dominate, there are good examples of Byzantine, Renaissance revival and art deco on Panepistimiou. The dream of a palace on the Acropolis, of magnificent archaeological theme parks unblemished by any occupants in their small houses, and of a formal city laid out along radiating boulevards as in Haussmann's Paris, never quite came true. But in Panepistimou it came close.

Leaving Syntagma, the best architecture is almost entirely to the right. Running parallel to Panepistimiou, Stadiou to the west and Akademias to the east also have some fine institutions, including (on Stadiou) the **National Historical Museum** and the **City of Athens Museum**.

The first outstanding mansion on leaving Syntagma is on the right-hand side at Panepistimiou 12 and it currently houses the **Numismatic Museum**. The coins are a world-famous collection but this is not the only museum in Athens where it is the building itself that is essential viewing. Iliou Megathron, the Palace of Troy (the inscription still survives) was built by the German architect Ziller for Heinrich Schliemann, the amateur archaeologist, Hellenophile and excavator of Mycenae, Tiryns and Troy. It was built in 1878, in a style inspired by Renaissance architecture ('an incurable leprosy,' sneered Kaftanzoglou). Side on to the street, its two steep and curving stairways rise to a main entrance that faces a courtyard and a statue of a nubile Amazon. The interior of this edifice, with mosaics and murals depicting scenes from the life of the hero-archaeologist, lives up to the promise of the exterior. Ziller

Buildings on Panepistimiou

Schliemann's House

continued to be of service to Schliemann, building a tomb for him to inhabit in equivalent and more permanent grandeur at the Proto Nekrotafio (Walk 8).

In the arcade at Panepistimiou 10, immediately before the Palace of Troy and slightly stranded at the far end of a row of mostly empty shops, is a fairly new addition to Athenian restaurants: *Cellier Le Bistrot*. Owned by a long-established wine merchant, this is a smart, well-run restaurant, French in inspiration, Greek in execution. It offers imaginative snacks as well as larger dishes. Snacks and main courses alike owe their inspiration to Greek food, but Greek food reinterpreted and beautifully presented: swordfish with pea purée, silver bream with basil, mountain cheese dipped in walnut flour and fried with sesame seeds, ice cream with sweet quince preserve. A great attraction here is that – rare in Greece – wines by the glass are available. This is an excellent opportunity to explore increasingly impressive Greek varieties and vintages, with the advice of a knowledgeable sommelier.

The mood here is of an idealized post-war era; the celebrity photographs are mostly of Churchill – in and out of cars, ruins, groups of earnest Greek politicians. A ceiling fan rotates slowly over marble tables, solid chairs and darkly varnished wood while a vast chandelier of crystal pear drops – amber and tangerine, ochre, russet and gold – hovers not far above the pristine black and white floor tiles; it has shades of the Metropolis.

Between Omirou and Sina on the right, both the Italian-style **Roman Catholic Cathedral of St Denis** (a.k.a. Dionysios) and the Byzantine-influenced eye hospital were designed by the versatile Kaftanzoglou. The **Academy of Athens** with its statue of Athena at her most implacable is pure classical homage. It was modelled largely on the Erechtheion, with details taken from the Temple of Apollo at Bassae and an approach copied from the Propylaia. The pediments have relief carvings of Athena and Apollo while Socrates and Plato sit, guardians of knowledge, either side of the entrance. Even the paintwork is intended to be true to ancient colours. It is possibly the finest neoclassical building anywhere; splendid if daunting in its marble, gold, deepest red and rich blue.

Next to the Academy are two further buildings in the same mood: the **National University** and the **National Library**. A long portico gives the university enormous grace and the murals inside the portico include attractive embodiments of all the subjects taught. Although the various departments of the modern institution are now scattered all over the city, the University building has great symbolic power, remaining in use as an administrative centre and for some formal ceremonies but, crucially, as the embodiment of learning at the centre of Greek culture.

The statues standing in front of the Old University form an incongruous fellowship. The British Prime Minister William Ewart Gladstone, the Independence hero Count John Capodistrias, the murdered patriarch of Constantinople Gregorious V, the executed radical poet Constantine Pheraios and the philosopher Adamantios Korais sit or stand together in this ordered spot with its lawns and palm trees. Together they express all the virtues that the new Greek state took to its bosom, just as the buildings around them express the values of a civilized nation to its people. The last of these great edifices, the National Library, was designed by Hansen as a Doric temple and it is still in use today.

When Alaric and his whole army came to the city, he saw the tutelary goddess Athena walking about the wall, looking just like her statue, armed and ready to resist attack, while leading their forces he saw the hero Achilles, just as Homer described him at Troy when in his wrath he fought to avenge the death of Patroclus. These apparitions were too much for Alaric who, giving up his attempt against the city, sent heralds to treat for peace.

Zosimus: *New History*, trans. Ronald Ridely.
(Sixth century CE.)

Opposite this constellation of neoclassical brilliance is an open plaza between Panepistimiou and Stadiou, known as **Korai**. Its bright, wide and unremarkable space contains one of the entrances to Panepistimiou metro and some welcome benches; otherwise it is largely a conduit for businessmen and women cutting between the two main roads. The impact of its only exceptional architecture, the **Demetrios Rallis Mansion** on the corner, is achieved largely by the conjunction of this low ochre and marble house with the towering office building that looms over it, its great expanse of glass appearing to move with the clouds it reflects.

However, there is one darker piece of history in Korai. Under the *Asty* cinema to the left is the basement once used as a Nazi interrogation chamber. It still exists, and not just in long Athenian memories, but it is rarely open to the public. A memorial plaque marks the location.

The right-hand side of Panepistimiou may overawe (as it was intended to), but the left side has its own, though subtle, treasures too. Arched entrances between a street front of rather grey financial institutions and offices give onto **arcade** after arcade, full of small shops, cafés and restaurants.

The arcade is a gentler homage to antiquity. Its form and function go back to the earliest *agora* and it has never been bettered. These examples are redolent of the more celebrated 'passages' in Paris. Dark and heavy – what natural light there is is filtered through frosted-glass roofs supported on iron ribs – they have a cool and slightly shabby *fin de siècle* air. All kinds of shops are hidden in them, from chemists to jewellers to electrical stores and the main office for the Athens Festival in the Spyromiliou Gallery, reached from both Panepistimiou and Stadiou.

But this whole area is above all a book-lovers' dream, from the superstores of Stadiou and Panepistimiou to the cramped shelves in the alleys of Exarchia. On Ipokratous every second shop seems to sell textbooks and the perennially restless can settle in with maps and travellers' tales at *Road Editions* at number 39. At Mavromihali 46, *Andromeda* specializes in classical history and archaeology, as does the *Archaeological Book Service* at Panepistimiou 57, which also has some unusual posters and cards. *Xenoglosso Vivliopoleio* at Ipokratus 10–12 has editions in four non-Greek languages. There are second-hand stalls on Solonos and Kalidromiou, in Exarchia, and spontaneously on many street corners; next to the fast-food outlets are fast-book shops. Most stock English-language books, often a remarkably broad selection. The Panepistimiou branch of

The Arcade of Books

the wonderful *Eleftheroudakis* spreads over seven floors at Panepistimiou 17, while *Kauffman* at Stadiou 28 specializes in English and French editions.

To the left, off Panepistimiou, Pesmazoglou leads to Sofokleous and the Athens Stock Exchange, but also to the charming **Stoa Orfeos**. Walking down its airy spaces, you turn along the wonderful **Stoa Bibliou**, the Arcade of Books, – an arcade within an arcade – which runs through to Stadiou. This marvel unfolds inside the **Arsakeio Building**, distinctive in white stone, classical motifs and dull silver cupolas; its commission was fought over by Kaftanzoglou and Kleanthis, its extension is by Ziller. It was once the national printing works and one great printing press still sits at the centre of its arcades.

At basement level in the Arsakeio is the once avant-garde Art Theatre. Above it, bookshop after bookshop, Greek publishers, a rolling exhibition, a café and a grand piano that draws surprising numbers of people to impromptu performance. Occasionally more formal concerts are held. Around all this, quiet corridors of volumes stretch off in every direction.

Music shops are here too. *Tzina* at Panepistimiou 57 has Greek music and bargains across the entire range. The largest in all Greece is *Metropolis*, at Panepistimiou 64, another cultural superstore: five storeys of tapes and CDs in a building that is much older than it might appear. It was for decades a Russian Patisserie – *The Rossikon*. Today its raw metal, rough stone and glass exterior is hung under a roof and from an iron-girdered structure first put up in 1910. Traditional instrument shops are becoming rare but *Pandora*, at Mavromihali 51, has lovely handmade stock.

The grandeur of Panepistimiou declines as it curves towards Omonia. Older guidebooks still advise the reader to take care on approaching the commercial heart of the city. It adds a certain frisson to what is otherwise simply a brash, untidy city centre. In Omonia everything has traditionally been up for sale. At night hopeful men scour the area, though the only 'women' loitering are taller, more heavily muscled and more exquisitely made-up than their more conventional sisters. Brothels are always said to be on the next corner. In reality what is invariably on the next corner is another airline office or travel agent's or car-hire outlet.

Omonia Square was always full of travellers. In its heyday it was the location of the best hotels catering to the influx of foreign tourists. Here were the nineteenth-century *Bangeion*, the *Alexander the Great*, the *Carleton*, the *Excelsior*, the *Plaza*: superior names that fitted the aspirations of this elegant circular space. Omonia, originally named Othonos after King Otto, was renamed Harmony Square after he was deposed. Over the decades it drifted towards a less-than-harmonious period. From the 1950s it became run-down and increasingly a legend, especially among foreigners, for danger and criminality.

Undoubtedly Omonia is cleaner and safer now. Many of the old hotel buildings have been restored to an echo of their glory days, regaining their handsome exteriors – although their interiors have been destroyed to make way for offices, the traffic has been controlled and the extensive building works for the new metro have simply disrupted whatever opportunistic lifestyle was previously led here. Curious visitors may lurk, looking for the dark Athenian underbelly, but they do so largely in vain – although they might still have their wallet lifted as they wait.

Omonia has two populations: itinerants, rising from the metro, buying their fast food, booking their way out of Athens; and immigrants, establishing a toehold in business. Cafés extrude their tables into the crush and even the pavements are carved up: the shoeshine boy, the leather-coats stall, the mobile-phone-card salesman. All of them shout: the tourists lost, cross, perplexed or demanding, the locals chewing the fat, negotiating, exasperated or threatening.

Like Monastiraki, Omonia is more richly multicultural than most other parts of Athens and this is one of the few districts where cuisine introduced by an ethnic minority can be found and enjoyed, usually very cheaply. One Chinese restaurant has small paper cups that, filled with water, reveal erotic pictures. Slow discovery is the mood of the Chinese restaurants and of the silk and herb shops of the embryonic **Chinatown** around the Athens Stock Exchange in Sofokleous and on Menandrou. Here too are tiny Indian and Pakistani restaurants (*Nargis* is the real thing, up a small alley on Sofokleous), barbers and fabric sellers and the intricacies of the Asian Neilos market, while African fruit stalls, music shops and grocers cluster in Geraniou.

Of Omonia's many small restaurants and cafés, one of the

best and most traditional is *Athenaikon*, founded in 1932 at
Themistokleous 2. Under the pre-war photographs of Athens,
the adventurous or the hungry eat 'stuffen spleen', drunkard's
titbits or 'galeos fried', served at marble-topped tables and
accompanied by solid country bread and robust table wine.
The less courageous have salad and *stiffado*. Offal is ascribed
legendary properties in this area, largely because of its alleged
restorative effect after alcohol. As in so many cities the best
offal restaurants, like this one, are only minutes away from
the meat markets or the abattoir.

Themistokleous continues towards **Exarchia**, quietly
interesting, neither over-restored nor crumbling into the dust:
a typical older Athenian street going about its low-key
business. At number 69 an impressive conversion of a
neoclassical house into a small theatre – *Theatre Exarchia* –

Tango

is worth pausing for. It may even, possibly, be worth attending a performance, usually a classical production in Greek. On the exterior the fine lines have been restored, the detail of antefixes, pediments and balconies picked out in contrasting colours. Inside is a marvellous dramatic space.

Themistokleous leads into Plateia Exarchion, very obviously the heart of the student quarter. It is like *any* student quarter, in any city in Europe. The numerous cafés, the alternative papers, the untidiness and the young inhabitants mark it out. The road continues, eventually, into Kalidromiou before ending at **Strefi Park**, another of Athens's welcome green spaces and sudden hills. On Saturday one of the city's best markets sprawls along here, between the cafés and the bars, of which *Milos* and *Café Kallidromiou* are two of the best.

Exarchia is inelegant, witty and energetic. Pockets of gentrification are springing up; the neoclassical-style houses that are being restored are simply retrieving their quieter residential past. The careless youthful charm that pervades Exarchia's back streets and small squares is not entirely uncontrived. Buildings here are painted, as they are in many places in Athens, but in tones that bear little resemblance to the well-researched pastel and earth colours of Plaka and Thissio. Here are dark reds, purples, citric green and, always, black. Every free surface is covered with the swirls and lightning of graffiti, unclaimed walls are textured with the energetic neglect of the just-passing-through, poles are feathered with peeling posters, decaying or mutilated, one on top of another. Destroy capital, tango, junkie enemas, PASOK. Stop the War stickers, Stop Israel, Stop Arsing Round. Doors have – still – painted hammers and sickles, flyers for clubs, cheap housing or body piercing.

Every house is in multiple occupation, rows of buzzers with single names: Drago, FiFi, Selim, Laz. Rubbish in every doorway, rubbish in the street, loud music and unforgiving streams of students in a hurry. *Fastfoodadika*, cafés, bars, music shops, barricaded clubs waiting for night, and then the peace of occasional benches: canvases for the master of the marker pen and the Swiss army knife, beds for the homeless or the out-of-it.

And more bookshops, silent and serious. They take little trouble with displays here; torn-open boxes of Cambridge University Press books, their titles in Greek, their instructions for box care in English, at length, block a doorway. In other shops convention dictates that pages are turned to a grimy shop window and title spines to the inside of the shop. One shop specializes in psychology and neuroscience, another in computer studies. These are serious dispensers of essential knowledge to those with exams to pass or teach.

The computer area around Stournari has the slightly depressing, well-lit utilitarianism that marks pc outlets everywhere, with a uniquely Greek spin of combined commercial pragmatism and disorder. Windows reveal congealing *café frappé* in plastic cups, motorbikes against window displays, international names: A ple, IBM, M cros ft, with crucial letters missing in an illuminated display, cables in serpentine heaps. In the war Stournari had a more sinister connection. Here were the SS headquarters, close to what is still the intellectual heart of the city.

This has always been a traditionally radical area. In 1973 the violence that followed the students' confrontation with the Colonels' Junta precipitated at least twenty-three deaths – extraordinarily, the true number remains unknown – and many hundreds of injuries at the **Polytechnic University**.

The courage of the 17 November protesters has been given a subsequent lethal memorial: the terrorist group that adopted the date as their name has been responsible for several deaths of British and American embassy and military personnel, although recent convictions seem to have ended the group's activities. The students now at university in Athens are the sons and daughters of those who faced the tanks, the beatings and the interrogations a quarter of a century ago. How can they make their own mark, be more extreme than parents who made history?

The tank continued its advance, I was caught up in the backward surge. I was running, hands thrust in the pocket of my overcoat, I could hear myself sobbing – like the howling of an animal. I tried to take refuge deep in myself. Outside the Engineering Faculty I crumpled to my knees in a corner and wept. Someone turned to me and said, hold up there, comrade. I scrambled to my feet and stood up straight. I took my hands out of my pockets and sorted out my hair. I could see the tank, its barrel levelled at the Faculty of Architecture.

Maro Douka: *Fool's Gold* (1991)

Next to the late nineteenth-century building of the Polytechnic University stands the **National Archaeological Museum** at 28 Oktovriou (metro: Viktoria). In summer, opening hours are Tues–Sun 8.00–19.00, Mon 12.30–19.00. In winter, Tues–Fri 8.00–15.00, Mon 11.00–15.00, Sat/Sun 8.30–15.00. It is without question one of the world's great collections. Housed in an immensely impressive neoclassical building, it has shared the vicissitudes of its city. During the war its precious artefacts were hidden and the museum only really recovered in the early 1960s. The earthquake of 1999 damaged both the museum and its collection. Its treasures are what you would expect from a country with a heritage as diverse and as rich in material remains as Greece, and at least a couple of hours are needed to complete even the most selective tour.

There are displays from every period in history and from all over the country and among them are some that astonish with the shock of the familiar. The funerary mask from Mycenae – the face of a long-dead king finely carved in gold – the marble Cycladic figurine of a harp player, the cup of Nestor, the fresh blue, ochre and terracotta of the fresco *Woman of Mycenae*, painted 1,500 years ago, the perfect bronzes and the statues of Poseidon and of those paradigms of male and female beauty, Antinous and Aphrodite.

Leaving the museum late, the best local restaurant (dinner only) is *Alexandreia* at Metsovou 13. This calm space offers Egyptian cuisine and is (appropriately) a reminder of Greece's ancient connections with that country. Wonderful flavours, especially of lamb, pulses and spiced food. Or assemble your own feast of authentic Greek food at **Gonia tou Agroti**. (Take Iraklio down the far side of the Museum and turn left at Kalidromiou at number 94, on the corner with Plapouta.) Here are the best flavours, textures and delicacies from all over Greece: fat dried beans, every imaginable herb, salt from Missolonghi, olives, little-known cheeses, biscuits and fine wine.

From this point there are several routes to Kolonaki. The least strenuous is to return to Omonia and then take the train to Syntagma, walking broadly east along Vassilissis Sofias for about 400 metres before turning left up Koumbari, past the Benaki Museum to Kolonaki Square. Alternatively, quite a long walk – 1,800 metres or so – in a south-easterly direction from the museum follows back streets through **Neapolis**. Neapolis, literally 'new town', is in fact a very old new town indeed, a residential area second only in age to Plaka. Its streets rise up the foothills of Mount Lykavittos, many of them with steps and handrails. It is an appealing area for no real reason, just more bookshops, blocks of apartments, leafy intersections, bright balconies and families making their way up or down the slopes.

A third option is to walk from Omonia down Akademias, passing the **Olympia Theatre** which houses Athens's opera house and ballet company. Further along Akademias is the **City of Athens Cultural Centre**. The building has a dignified simplicity, particularly by contrast with the classical extravaganza in front of it. The formal white lines of this two-storey building were once those of the city's original municipal hospital, built in 1836. It has a café with an entrance off Solonas and sells books on every conceivable aspect of the city but it is primarily a useful but little-known organizer of free tours of Athens.

The Academy, Panepistimiou

Within the complex is a **Museum of Theatre**. Exhibiting atmospherically lit sets and dressing rooms, authentically glittering and tawdry, it displays costumes, memorabilia, photographs and sketches for productions. It is a museum that might seem to be more of interest to those (few) familiar with the Greek theatre in the twentieth century, yet it triumphs in recreating the universally hectic, thrilling and sensuous mood of the stage. But of course drama was born here, in Athens, and still dominates its culture; there are over 120 theatres in the city. This small museum traces that extraordinary heritage and an enduring Greek passion for the stage and for glamour, from shadow puppets and the costumes of antiquity to, inevitably, Maria Callas and Melina Mercouri.

A diversion up Voukourestiou is for the sweet-toothed; it too is, in its way, a museum of nostalgia, one where the past is for purchase and consumption. At number 11, *Caravan* is a legendary *siropiasta* (patisserie). Here are feather-light pastries, sweet and savoury, filigree concoctions of honey and nuts, crystal webs of sugar, and some wonderfully strange and unfamiliar tastes and combinations.

Return to Akademias, eventually taking an oblique left-hand turn up Kanari which also leads swiftly to Plateia Kolonakiou.

Guidebooks and its residents proclaim **Kolonaki** the Mayfair of Athens. Although the houses are expensive and set in the secure compounds of the wealthy urban dweller, it is a long time since Kolonaki was truly chic. The rich prefer to live nearer the coast or in the outer garden suburbs, the Bohemians in Psirri.

Yet the Plateia and its surrounding avenues retain a certain self-conscious style in the anticipation of celebrity; one café creates its own microclimate of fine, cooling mist, the seats are invariably full and the riffs and trills of a hundred mobile phones pierce the subdued but constant beat of rock music. In the kitchens of Kolonaki, a hundred *café frappés* – the glutinous rehydrated packet mix that has only ever caught on in Greece and Malaysia – are whisked into froth.

Up Skoufa, to the north-west, is *Ta Tria Gourounakia* (the Three Little Pigs). Porcine pink inside, it is the essence of Kolonaki for daytime snacks, coffee or fashionable late-night eating and dancing. The easily bored are entertained even into the lavatories, which claim to be restorations of the straw, wood and brick houses of the ancient pigs. Each cubicle now has its own DVD show.

The square's official name is Plateia Filikis Etairias, after the secret society that fomented revolt against the Turks in 1821. It became Kolonaki to those who patronized it because a column fragment – found in Dexameni Square, and probably part of Hadrian's reservoir – has sat here since 1958 (about the same time the *frappé* arrived, invented by a desperate Nestlé salesman). The **British Council** has its headquarters here. Independence rebels or not, this has, from the start, been a middle-class neighbourhood.

In the garden of the Plateia are three statues whose awkward conjunction, styles and subject matter expose the delightfully complicated legacy of heritage. A severe island revolutionary surmounts an ancient herm, one of the founders of the secret society gazes into eternity, and a modern faceless, beaked goddess, with one wing and the hips and bad legs of a *yiayia*, sits strumming – without arms – on a mandolin.

Busy Patriarhi Ioakim goes off towards the north-east from Kolonaki. Turning left from it into Loukianou, **Lykavittos** lies ahead, the conical, southernmost peak in the range of the Turkovounia mountains. It is a demanding climb. Away from the square there are plenty of funky boutiques – clever window dressing, solitary and beautiful ephemera, distinguished fashionable names – but there are no *periptero* here and few cafés on the steep and quiet streets that lead towards Lykavittos Hill: slender profit margins are not for wealthy areas.

On a hot day a quiet desperation can set in here, struggling upwards under the plump trees and closed shutters of well-maintained and impregnable houses. *O Kafenion* at Loukianou 26 has excellent food, a sort of Kolonaki take on *mezhedes* with a sophisticated wine list, but its name can only be ironic. This is no café. Smooth men with fat cigars broker deals over lunch at heavy-linened tables, women with fragile high heels can never have negotiated this or any other hill. Fiscal virtue is put to the test; the shade of the umbrellas on the pavement is almost irresistible at any price.

It is easier, and perhaps more fun, to take **the funicular** by turning up Ploutarhou, one road after Loukianou. Alternatively, it is possible to come directly into the area by metro from Syntagma and get off at Evangelismos. The train is full of silent medical students, deep in the unspeakable pages of their textbooks, highlighters held like scalpels and an air of dread and imminently approaching examination. The station has good archaeological displays and a striking piece of modern iron sculpture by Chrysa.

Outside, Evangelismos is a large state hospital, which was founded by an international arms dealer turned great philanthropist. Vassilis Zaharof emerged from the First World War a enormously wealthy and much-decorated man, with a Spanish duchess for a wife and a British knighthood for a reputation. As well as the Evangelismos, he provided marble for the stadium and funding for the Polytechnic and several schools. His will provided funds for, more appropriately, a warship.

Coming out of the station into a small park, cross Vassilissis Sofias and head north of the hospital along Gennadiou. The seventeenth-century complex on the right is Moni Petraki, a theological college with medical origins. It was founded by a doctor member of the order so that he could practise his profession in Athens. Gennadiou leads into Souidias, a pretty street whose air is sweet with the orange trees that provide its shade. Both the **British School of Archaeology** and the **American School of Classical Studies** are here but the centrepiece of this oasis of learning is the striking **Gennadion Library** at Souidias 61.

Built in the 1920s, in classical style, its dark red stucco, white columns and green topiary are extremely handsome. John Gennadius was a different sort of benefactor. A businessman and diplomat, a Greek who lived in London, he gave some 27,000 books on Greek topics to the American School of Classical Studies, who in their turn built this library to contain them. Gennadius was not a rich man – indeed, when he died in 1932 he still owed money to various bookshops – but he was a lifelong bibliophile and a passionate Hellenist. This passion created a book collection that has become the single greatest source for Greek and Byzantine works. The subsidiary items here make it a museum of Philhellenism as much as a library. Those wishing to use the books have to apply in advance but the other items in the Gennadion can be seen every day except Sunday.

The delightful atmosphere and position of the library alone are worth a detour. The art here includes more than 200 of Edward Lear's evocative watercolour sketches of nineteenth-century Greece. The archive of Byron memorabilia includes his last watercolour portrait, showing his dog, Lion, and his Souliot guards. Perhaps most moving of all, here too is the wreath of laurel leaves and flowers sent by the people of Missolonghi, where Byron died, to lie on the poet's body in

London. The personal papers of poets George Seferis and Odysseas Elytis and of the archaeologist Heinrich Schliemann are among others kept at the Gennadion. Above the entrance are inscribed the words: 'They are Greeks who share in our culture.'

●

I rented a studio apartment with a terrace just off the Lycabettus ring road, near the Navy hospital. In the day my view consisted of television antennas and dirty rooftops; at night all I could see were small cells of electricity in various shades.

Neni Eftimiadi: 'The Courier', from D. Sughart,
Athens by Neighbourhood (2001)

●

Continue along the road, with the library to the right, and turn along Ploutarhou for the funicular. The cabin rises with vertiginous speed, a recorded voice welcoming the upwardly mobile to 'this divine, fresh place' with bursts of the inevitable 'Never on Sunday'.

The funicular burrows up the rock to emerge at the foot of Ag. Georgios, a nineteenth-century white chapel which claims Lykavittos for Christianity. Mythologically it was said that Lykavittos was formed by the goddess Athena who, startled by a crow bearing bad news, dropped a boulder she was carrying from the Penteli mountains (long a source of more conventional mining) on her way to the Acropolis to form the citadel. A quote from Revelations 15 is carved into the rock in Greek and English to clear this up: *'Great and wonderful are Thy deeds, oh Lord God Almighty. Who shall not fear and glorify Thy name?'*

While in antiquity this was just a barren crag, today it is covered in trees and the area smells of aromatic pine resin.

There is invariably a light breeze up here, a flag flutters, its wires snap against the pole and birds hover on thermals high above the peak. In spring the hillsides are briefly covered with wild cyclamen and it is a favourite place (there is not much choice) for Athenians to pick the traditional blooms for the 1 May wreath that hangs on every door. Later in the summer, bushy shrubs tremble with butterflies, and in the evening the sky is crossed by swifts. Even in winter, the hill retains its distinctive dark green cover and crows still go about their business. An expensive restaurant sells good food and a leisurely view and its associated café has wonderful fresh fruit juices and ice cream, a range – not extensive – of 1970s pop songs and one of the best lavatories in the city.

Until 1941, Lykavittos was the strategically crucial stronghold of Greek Air Force operations and it was, in its way, a last stand, where King George held out before accepting the inevitability of the German advance and leaving the mainland for Crete. Nowadays, beyond its natural beauty, there is little to see *up* Lykavittos – although there is a popular open-air theatre at one end – but everything to see *from* it. There are telescopes on a viewing platform, heavily ornamented with the mark of the hill-climbing graffitist.

Slightly higher than the Acropolis, the view from here is superb – at least when the day is clear. From up here Athens makes sense. The Acropolis is somehow diminished and unreal from this perspective but the city around it is vast. It stretches as far as the mountains in one direction, with Mount Hymettus to the south-east, unfolding towards the Saronic Gulf and its islands: Salamis, Hydra, Poros and Aegina. On the best days the distant Peloponnese rises along the horizon. On bad days a relentless grey vista of apartment blocks, offices, aerials and satellite dishes fades into a hazy sea of smog. Athens's notorious *nefos* is now officially vanquished but the relative success of anti-pollution laws is being eroded by the growth in car ownership. In addition, the massive works for the 2004 Olympics – building sites, roads, quarries, open-topped lorries – released high levels of dust into the air.

○

At a vigorous pace they breasted the hillside, turning often to gaze at the dazzling whiteness of Athens below them and at the wondrous panorama spreading around as they ascended. On reaching the quarries Louis pointed with indignation to the girls and women who toiled at breaking stone. 'That's the kind of thing that makes me detest these countries!'

'What about cotton mills and match factories?' said Langley. 'It's better breaking stone on Lycabettus.'

George Gissing: *The Sleeping Fires*, 1895

○

Descend to Kolonaki by the many shady paths and resting places and then, by turning right on Vassilissis Sofias, walk back to Syntagma.

After the Acropolis, Lykavittos is the most constant landmark in Athens, suddenly appearing at the end of streets or over the roof of an apartment block, its small church illuminated on a summer night. But it is at its loveliest seen from below at Easter when the Resurrection is marked by a candlelit procession, which starts at the chapel and winds its way down the hill in the darkness. In this service of Epitafios, Christ's symbolic bier is brought down from the heights to the city. It is an unforgettable sight.

Houses, an embassy, the hospital,
Our neighbourhood sun-cured if trembling still
In pools of the night's rain . . .
Across the street that led to the centre of town
A steep hill kept one company part-way
Or could be climbed in twenty minutes
For some literally breathtaking views,
Framed by umbrella pines, of city and sea.
Underfoot, cyclamen, autumn crocus grew
Spangled as with fine sweat among the relics
Of good times had by all. If not Olympus,
An out-of-earshot, year-round hillside revel.

James Merrill: *Days of 1964*

THE SEVENTH WIND

East

Apeliotes

*Bearing flowers and
fruit in his light cloak*

- The shade and cafés of the Zappion and National Gardens
- The museums of Vassilissis Sofias
- The Parliament building and the Tomb of the Unknown Soldier
- The Hotel Grande Bretagne
- Syntagma Square
- The Metro

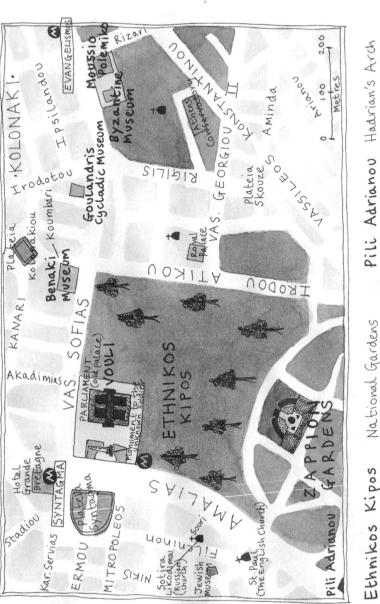

Ethnikos Kipos   National Gardens   Pili Adrianou   Hadrian's Arch

Moussio Polemiko   Athens   War Museum

In a crowded city of long, hot summers, it is not ruins or fine mansions that bring most pleasure to those who live there but the luxury of natural shade. It is the paucity of gardens or parks that makes the dense housing of the Athens suburbs seem remorseless. The water constantly running down street gutters on the hottest days is draining from the carefully nurtured balcony pot plants that are all many city dwellers possess in the way of a garden.

Wherever a few limes or planes grow on a street corner there are Athenians chatting on a bench. Shade offers protection, sociability and sensual pleasure. In central Athens, parks are not so much an indulgence as an alternative existence. Long before air-conditioning, parks had become great outdoor rooms, dark, dense, cool and peaceful. Today hoses coil, serpentine, into the bushes, nurturing precious trees, and the green spaces are still an escape from the climate and overcrowding of the capital.

In the 1830s, as Greece emerged in muddled triumph from the overturning of Turkish domination, the young German prince Otto (whose father King Ludwig I of Bavaria was a committed Philhellene and classical archaeologist, and largely controlled the decisions of his son) was imposed upon them. Otto's consort, Amalia, finding herself in a country very different from the temperate and disciplined land of her youth, demanded shade appropriate to a queen. In the 1840s Amalia's gardeners and botanists began to lay out the beautiful Royal Gardens adjacent to what was then the Royal Palace. Today there are 7,000 trees and around 40,000 plant species growing here; some, pampered and protected, have reached extraordinary size. At the time it was seen as an outrageous expenditure and did little to enhance the couple's precarious popularity, and even before the king was deposed, concessions that allowed the public to walk in the gardens when the royal family were elsewhere had been *instigated. Queen Amalia never saw the maturity of the specimen trees she had brought from Italy but her legacy has been a great, if inadvertent, gift to Athens.*

●

> ... The Queen wished to surround herself with shade, perfumes and bright colours, and the song of birds – what she asked for has been given her.
> Those who have passed three summer months in Greece know that the most precious good, and the one most worthy of being sought for, is shade – in the royal garden there are thickets where the sun never penetrates. The king's dining room is a room under the open sky. Surrounded by open galleries; the sides and roof are of climbing rose-trees.

Edmond About, 1852

●

Starting at **Hadrian's Arch**, cross over Vassilissis Olgas to enter the National Gardens at their south-western end. In May and June the avenue of jacaranda trees is a feathery haze of pink and the reds, oranges and purples of subtropical flowers persist throughout the summer heat, bright against the evergreen foliage. *The Oasis* restaurant is only one shrubbery's width away from the main road and is a favourite lingering place for escapees from the dusty street. There has been a café here for decades and at *Oasis* people still rest at little metal tables, deep in the trees, attended by a middle-aged waiter dressed as he might have been at any time in the last century.

The gardens – **Ethnikos Kipos** – are not large enough to get lost in, yet even on this perimeter where they run alongside one of Athens's busiest avenues they provide an almost instant change of pace and atmosphere and era. Only sixty years ago this lush retreat from the dry heat of Athens was a battle zone as bloody exchanges of fire took the Greek civil war to the heart of the city. But to Athenians now the park is synonymous with sensual pleasures: eating, sleeping, love. Young couples are entwined in each other's arms in glades, older and more illicit ones sit intense and low-voiced over their coffees at a café table. Office workers escape and sleep under trees, mothers let their children loose, clusters of old men are a committee of advice over a backgammon board. Solitary visitors with time on their hands linger over books or papers on benches in what are virtually alfresco reading rooms – long pergolas heavy with plumbago and jasmine. It is the perfect secret garden.

In 1870 the wealthy Zappas cousins laid out a more formal park adjacent to the existing gardens and erected the handsome formal mansion, **the Zappion**, now used as a conference centre. When not busy with dignitaries and flags and despite its immaculate exterior and excellent *Aigli*

National Gardens

restaurant, the Zappion feels a little forgotten. Too large and perfect for its site, it is a landmark rather than a destination. Yet in Lent it comes to life. As Athenians fly kites fly on the crest of Philopappus across the old city, in the Zappion, where the trees are budding, hundreds of children in fancy dress gather around its steps, and bands and stalls selling masks, lollipops and metallic balloons fill the gardens under a bright and unstable early spring sky.

●

> I walked about enchanted on this first night in Zappion. It remains in my memory like no other park I have known. It is the quintessence of park, the thing one feels sometimes in looking at a canvas or dreaming of a place you'd like to be in but never find. It is lovely in the morning too as I was to discover. But at night, coming upon it from nowhere, feeling the hard dirt under your feet and hearing a buzz of language which is altogether unfamiliar to you, it is magical—

> Henry Miller: *The Colossus of Maroussi* (1941)

●

Today the whole area exists in a state of wonderful profusion, conveying a sense that the gardeners are just and only just keeping it all under control. A notice warns passers-by to beware the 'unexpected' fall of trees. Here a tumbled column lies in long grass, there a rustic bridge or the statue of a stern and forgotten statesman is almost subsumed into the undergrowth. Tall, weeping trees have reached out and become entangled overhead, while hand-painted wooden signs lure explorers up narrow paths to a delightfully improbable collection of amenities: a children's library, a carp pond, a botanical museum.

Wandering up and down the paths, you can find the ruins of a Roman bath, King Otto's shooting box or an ancient conduit. A large ornamental lake, and most of the seats and rocks around it, is covered with relaxed Aylesbury ducks – smaller ponds are home to terrapins. There are cats everywhere: a great glossy family of huge cats asleep in bushes, on marble thrones, or in the shade of a stone angel.

Then there is the **zoo**. It is not one of Europe's great collections. Animals are rife in the decoration of Greek architecture. From the lions and bulls of antiquity to the

National Gardens

swans and griffins of nineteenth-century houses, Greek imagination takes flight with unfamiliar or entirely fantastic creatures. Reality is another matter. The zoo possesses two manic ostriches, a pair – unfortunately both male – of peacocks, and some empty and fortified cages that speak of savage beasts temporarily unavailable. The other exhibits here are pigeons (optimistically labelled 'doves'), rabbits, hens and (domestic) cats: creatures not unknown to any Greek with a back garden.

There is no one route through the park; in the spirit of its haphazard charms, it is best to wander at will – almost every visit throws up new discoveries. Although it is enclosed within railings, there are numerous exits and entrances. On the eastern side, by Irodou Atikou, is a notorious and delightful place for a rendezvous. The café, *O Kipos* (The Park), is set around a damp, mossy grotto, its small tables scattered in the dappled light of trellised alcoves. On Sundays the sound of military bands give this leisured spot a decidedly old-fashioned air.

●

What a thrill it had been, she'd been browsing round the shops in the centre of town, when she'd seen him standing before her like an answer to a prayer. They'd gone for a walk arm in arm, happy beyond words. They'd wound up at the Zappeion gardens and sat down at a patisserie. He'd said to her, let me read your palm. She asked him gaily what he saw. Telly had pursed his lips and kissed the hollow of her hand, I see a great love he'd said with a tremor in his voice.

Maro Douka: *Fool's Gold* (1991)

●

Turning left from the exit by the café brings you at right angles into Irodou Atikou, a beautiful street, wide and lined with tamarind, magnolia and orange trees, with mansions set back behind high gates and impenetrable gardens. Halfway up the street **Evzones** – the presidential bodyguard, seen on a hundred postcards and every tourist photograph – protect the presidential palace. Their history is a little murky but their ornamental beauty and gravitas now triumphs over the traditional bobble boots and unloaded guns (the real firepower lies with the armed police who guard the guards). Their smooth and substantial calves are bolstered with two pairs of white stockings and the 130 nails in boots designed to grip on perilous mountain terrain make walking on smooth city pavements a hazardous part of their duty.

●

Going for an afternoon stroll in the Zappeion Gardens, one unsuspecting pedestrian was caught up in the firing between a group of Evzones and their quarry, and shot in the stomach. The National Gardens, which verged on Constitution Square within sight of the Grande Bretagne hotel, turned into a jungle where gunmen stalked each other through the dense greenery.

Mark Mazower: Inside Hitler's Greece (1995)

Irodou Atikou leads into a T-junction with Vassilissis Sofias. This was once the Marathon road and has had several names in a long and chequered history, but its present style was developed after Greek independence. Sofias set out to be an elegant boulevard in the French style, running from the erstwhile palace – now the parliament building – towards Kolonaki. Several of Sofias's surviving villas, many now functioning as embassies, are indeed handsome. But it is in the main a dusty road, heavy with traffic, low on trees of any size. However, some of Athens's best museums lie on or immediately off Vassilissis Sofias and the trudge between them is more than rewarded by the cool beauty of their galleries.

Coming out of Irodou Atikou but remaining on the park side and turning right, the **Byzantine Museum** is at Vassilissis Sofias 22. This outstanding collection – reflecting the spirit as well as the glory of the age – is housed in the Villa Ilisia. Originally built for Sophie de Marbois-Lebrun, Duchesse de Plaisance, this lovely house once bordered the now vanished ancient **River Ilissus**. The Duchess was a sad as well as an eccentric figure, usually seen in her own version of Greek national dress and known for the salon of intellectuals that she gathered around her. Separated from her husband, one of Napoleon's generals, she had come to Greece after the death of her only child, bringing the coffin

The Byzantine Museum

with her. Her first house was in Plateia Omonia and when it burned down it effectively cremated her daughter's corpse. Gathering the ashes, she moved to her new house on the Ilissus, where, it was rumoured, she talked to the remains as if the child was alive.

A little further along to the right, on the corner with Rizari, is Athens's War Museum, the **Moussio Polemiko** (Tues–Sat 9.00–14.00; Sun 9.30–14.00), housed, perhaps appropriately, in a bunker-like modern building. It is hard to miss because of the fighter plane and attendant small boys permanently stationed outside.

Turning back down Vassilissis Sofias, on the opposite side of the road is the **Goulandris Museum of Cycladic and Ancient Greek Art** (Mon, Wed–Fri 10.00–16.00; Sat 10.00–15.00), which is housed in the striking modern building by architect Yiannis Vikelas and a late nineteenth-century house – The Stathatos Mansion – designed by Ziller. (The entrance to the museum is at Neofytou Douka 4.) The gallery of Cycladic figurines – 350 marble images, usually of women, simple, still perplexing and deceptively modern in appearance – has long been the pre-eminent collection here but the recent display of the most significant finds from the excavations for the metro is also fascinating.

Continuing along Vassilissis Sofias towards Syntagma, the deliciously eclectic collections of the **Benaki Museum** (Mon, Wed, Fri, Sat 9.00–17.00; Thu 9.00–midnight; Sun 9.00–15.00) are displayed in what was once the Benaki family's private house. Having just emerged from years of restoration, the museum unfolds a Greek history told through its art and artefacts. It is a selective history: the Greek War of Independence is a high point of celebration, while the horrors of the 1940s – the Nazi occupation, the destruction of the Jewish communities, the famine, the post-war internecine fighting between Greek factions, and the years of the Junta – are virtually invisible.

But the history that *is* on show is wonderfully conveyed: whole interiors, elaborate costumes from every region of the country, outstandingly beautiful embroideries, icons, ornate metalwork and ceramics. The folk art of rural Greece, the European court dress and jewels of the elite, the weapons and words of her heroes, are all here. If Greece through Greek eyes is a refracted image, then the gallery of art produced by foreigners, largely by Grand Tourists, in response to the country provides an appealing and equally filtered shift of perspective. Chronologically the last exhibits are works and mementoes from twentieth-century writers and artists, most affecting when they are flimsy and tattered. Here too are the early drafts and Nobel Prizes of the poets George Seferis and Odysseas Elytis.

Strange people! They say they're in Attica but
    they're really nowhere;
They buy sugared almonds to get married
They carry hair tonic, have their photographs taken
The man I saw today sitting against a background
    of pigeons and flowers
Let the hands of the photographer smooth away the
    wrinkles
Left on his face
By all the birds in the sky.

George Seferis:
Wherever I travel Greece wounds me

It is possible at this point to head up Koumbari and enter Plateia Kolonakiou and the elegant streets that lead off it and even to climb flight after flight of steps to reach the cable car to Lykavittos (Walk 6). Alternatively, it is just five minutes' walk from the Benaki to **Syntagma ('Constitution') Square**. Vassilissis Sofias follows the northern edge of the National Gardens and comes into the square along the side of the formal, ochre-coloured parliament building, the **Vouli**. This handsome edifice was built between 1836 and 1842 as the Royal Palace for King Otto. In front of it Evzones guard the **Tomb of the Unknown Soldier**. The tomb itself is marked by a simple relief carving of a dying ancient warrior. In a clump of trees to the left, modern soldiers have set up their very small camp. Helmets hang on the branches, coffee is brewing, the soldiers play cards – apparently deaf to the roar of the traffic and the shutter-clicking of Evzone-worshipping tourists. The site of the Vouli was once known as the Place of Thunder. It still thunders, but with traffic, not the foaming cascade of a now-unimaginable spring.

The new palace is a very extensive building, much larger than a king of Greece can require for his residence, or than his household can fill. It is an oblong square, about ninety paces by seventy. I have not seen the plans, but for the present it looks as if rather intended for a barrack than for a royal palace.

Edgar Garston, 1840

Another palatial landmark was rising at the same time as the palace. **The Hotel Grande Bretagne**, an Athenian institution, is on the opposite corner, gleaming in its refurbishment, with limousines, apparently immune to city parking laws, drawn up in untidy rows, watched over by immaculate commissionaires, waiting chauffeurs and hot policemen on wide motorbikes. At the height of summer, for the price of an expensive drink, you can, in effect, buy an hour or so of air-conditioned comfort on one of the hotel lobby's vast sofas.

The *Grande Bretagne* is in a time zone of its own. It is a country of its own. It is certainly not Greece. Those who knew it in its faded prime regret the new gold leaf, the silks, the oriental carpets and the tessellated marble but they have an impressive opulence that might have gone down well with Herodes Atticus two thousand years ago. Metre-wide arrangements of blue and cream flowers stand on empire-style tables. (Nothing occasional about them; all is deliberation here.) A small tropical palm grove thrusts up to the light, a pianist ripples over the notes of a grand piano. It is perpetual early evening in the marble halls of the *Grande Bretagne*. Waitresses in black cheongsams move smilingly between the international businessmen, the ubiquitous politicians and the elegant hotel-enhancing women.

The thoughts of the most ardent Hellenophile drift into dissatisfaction and disloyalty. The constancy and quantity of the chandeliers; the perfection of the ambient temperature; the splendid lavatories and the depth of the upholstery suggest that such expertise could be available in the real world and that only perversity prevents it being so.

The *Grande Bretagne* has always been desirable. Originally a private house, it became a hotel of eighty bedrooms, served by just two bathrooms, in 1874. In the Second World War it was, successively, the headquarters of the Greek, the German and the British forces. In 1944 a bomb placed in the cellars nearly removed both the hotel and Winston Churchill who favoured an interventionist stance in the fight between nationalism and communism that followed the war. He had come to Athens to negotiate with the belligerents. His insistence on controlling the confrontation and on the suppression of left-wing extremists saw the British taking up arms against Greek 'terrorists', which led to the extraordinary sight of Spitfires strafing the Athenian suburbs and the gun emplacements on the Acropolis.

There is residual resentment today among some older Greeks who believe that British partisanship and subsequent withdrawal when the cost of involvement in Greece became too high, escalated the subsequent violence of the 1940s which became the foundation for the right-wing atrocities of later years. At this hotel one last attempt was made to deflect the British from their meddling.

Leaving the *Grande Bretagne* is always a shock. Heat radiates off its broad marble steps, traffic is relentless, deferential charm stops at the door; the crowds forced by the parked cars to walk in the road are in no mood to give way. Syntagma was always the traditional hub of the city. Now it offers something for everyone and, as a consequence, seems to miss being a place in its own right. It is a place of transition, of travellers, of people wanting to be somewhere else. A McDonald's stands virtually next to a *periptero*; taxis, buses and confused tourists create a congested and short-tempered world.

Yet Syntagma is not unattractive. The centre of the square has been revived around its new metro. What it has perhaps lost in chaotic charm it has gained in breathing space. Low hedges, pineapple palms and benches in the shade of plane trees offer a moment's respite for travellers about to descend into the metro, take the coach to the airport or bus to the suburbs, or move with disorientating speed into the quite different atmospheres of the major streets that radiate off the square. Vassilissis Sofias goes east. Ermou, running west eventually as far as the ancient cemetery of Athens at Keramikos, is a jangle of department stores and designer shops. To the north-west, Panepistimiou (Eleftherios Venizelou) is a street of dignity and learning; of the academy, the library, some of the greatest neoclassical buildings in the world and arcades of coffee houses and bookshops. (See Walk 6.)

In Zaharatos' old coffee shop
In Syntagma, in the back, in the corner,
A respectable Athenian, bent
Over, reflects on old times.

Fotos Yofyllis (1887–1981):
The Athenian's Sorrow

Filelinon (lovers of Greece), going almost due north, is not a particularly attractive street; its only celebrated site is the **Russian Church of Sotira Likodimou**, built on the remains of a second-century CE Roman baths (still visible but not always accessible). It is a bulky building but older than it looks –

probably the largest building surviving in Athens from the medieval period. It has been battered by history, ending up derelict after a succession of natural and man-made disasters until it was refurbished by the Russians in the mid-eighteenth century. Nearby is the **English church of St Paul**, an indifferent but unmistakably British building. Inside there are memorials to exiles who have come to grief in a foreign land at the hands of brigands or disease.

Nearby is succour of a more immediate kind. The charming, knowledgeable chemist at Filelinon 7 is an enthusiast on all matters pharmaceutical. He also carries wonderful body scrubs, shampoos and luxury creams mostly made from Greek ingredients – although white chocolate creeps in – and seductively packaged. He is an English-speaker, as happy to engage in a conversation on antihistamines or examine an unprepossessing blister as he is to press samples of unctuous bath oil upon his customers or to consider the merits of alternative medicine.

In Nikis – a minor street to the right – is the English language bookshop *Compendium*: 'a taste of a bookshop, the touch of a library' it proclaims, upstairs at number 28. This is a refuge for all longer-term foreign visitors. Its range of books is as broad and haphazard as that of any bookshop in an English university town: classical texts in translation, histories, potboilers, children's books and a wonderful selection of travel guides. Small notices offer language teaching, kittens, a room, courses in Gestalt therapy or modern Greek poetry.

Further consolation for the homesick traveller lies next door in a little wine shop carrying an unusual range of Greek produce and towards the far (Plaka) end of Nikis is the Jewish Museum (Walk 1).

The glory of Syntagma Square today is its metro. The Athens metro has been a notoriously long time in coming.

The city's failure to put an effective infrastructure in place was a principal reason why its bid for the 1996 Olympic was refused. Athenians were astonished, disappointed and, finally, galvanized. The seven years of disruption were horrendous but what emerged from behind the hoardings was an exemplary underground system. The Athens metro, though still quite small, can claim to be the best in Europe. The stations have the advantage of being brand new and they are maintained to an immaculate

Wine shop

standard, all wide marble concourses and stainless steel with, as yet, no graffiti and only one, frequently repeated, advertisement: a tanned female bottom, smooth as a statue's, proclaiming the advantages of depilation.

This is a metro system underground of cool air, classical music and education. The stations are museums of their own past, and galleries of modern art. Each has its own style: Omonia has collages of shadowy crowds and of footballers, shaped in tissue petals. On the platform, bronze doors like those of an ancient tomb and terracotta tiles pay glancing references to archaic Greece. At Panepistimiou ancient artefacts show the range of the archaeological finds and modern abstract sculptures in bronze and clay echo the ancient materials. The displays are a master stroke, simultaneously demonstrating the nation's sensitive and informed archaeology policies and justifying slow technological progress. At Akropolis, life-size reproductions

Sculpture at Syntagma metro

of the Parthenon friezes follow the platform walls and a
stunning photograph, looking like an inferno at first glance,
that was taken at the moment when the engineers broke
through into a Byzantine rubbish pit and a deluge of shards
and amphorae swept into the tunnel. Syntagma is the jewel
in the public-transport crown: eleven cases of discoveries
from the excavations include a skeleton, in front of which
beaming groups have their photographs taken for their
shared posterity. And then there is the light well. Viewed
from the bottom, Giorgos Zogolopoulos's work of art is a
luminous funnel to the sky; looking downwards from its
glass vault in the square itself, it is a wonderful fantasy of
rippling aluminium in which ladders and umbrellas are
suspended on filaments that sway with the movement of the
trains far below.

Like Pikionis's subtly perfect paths around the Acropolis and up the ancient city hills, the true glory of modern Athenian architectural design may lie in the transformation of the functional and the mundane into something beautiful and extraordinary.

THE EIGHTH WIND
South-East

Euros

An old man in a thick
cloak, bringing rain
and violent storms

- The Arch of Hadrian
- The Temple of Olympian Zeus
- The River Ilissus
- The Fix Brewery
- The nineteenth-century district of Mets
- The Athens First National Cemetery
- The Olympic Stadium

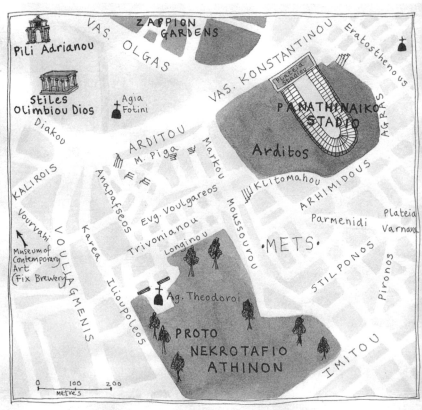

Pili Adrianou

ZAPPION GARDENS

VAS. OLGAS

VAS. KONSTANTINOU

Eratosthenous

Stiles Olimbiou Dios

Agia Fotini

Plateia Stadiou

PANATHINAIKO STADIO

Diakou

ARDITOU

M. Piga

Markou

Arditos

SARGA

KALIROIS

Anapafseos

Evg. Voulgareos

Klitomahou

ARHIMIDOUS

Parmenidi

Plateia Varnava

Vourvahi

VOULIAGMENIS

Karea

Trivonianou

Longinou

Moussourou

·METS·

STILPONOS

Pironos

Museum of Contemporary Art (Fix Brewery)

Ilioupoleos

Ag. Theodoroi

PROTO NEKROTAFIO ATHINON

IMITOU

0   100   200
metres

Stiles Olimbiou Dios   Temple of Olympian Zeus
Panathinaiko Stadio   Olympic Stadium

Pili Adrianou   Hadrian's Arc
Proto Nekrotafio   Cemetery

The sense of a missing river is something that slowly emerges as you get to know Athens. Unlike most other great cities there is no defining waterway, no embankment of grand houses, no pleasure cruisers, cranes and docks or distant morning boat horns signalling commercial waters. No conduit through the stone and marble and cement. (Of course Athens has a seaport, a huge one, at Piraeus, now absorbed into the city itself, and all Greeks constantly travel by water. One-fifth of their land mass is made up of islands: islands from which most Athenians still derive a strong sense of their roots.)

But still the city hints at water – if not an abundance, at least a sufficiency: trees grow tall; parks have grass soft enough to sleep on. Even at the height of summer, water still trickles down the gutters of most side streets: water from zealous car-washers fighting their unending war against dust; water from dripping air-conditioning units; water falling like rain from balconies bright with thirsty flowers.

Yet Athens has relatively few ponds, lakes or fountains. The famous ones in Omonia Square have been casualties of restoration, though fountains would be a welcome addition to the new schemes: on a hot day in Syntagma Square the summer crowds walking across the burning pavement swerve sinuously towards the fountain there, simply to let the fine spray fall upon them momentarily. And it is here, at the east end of this, the most important of Athens's squares, that one instinctively feels a river is going to appear: behind the parliament building, near the dense foliage of the National Gardens, passing across or alongside the elegant mansions of Vassilissis Sofias.

It doesn't. Vassilissis Sofias, for all its grandeur, is broad, hot and dry.

Yet once there were rivers in Athens. Interestingly, instinct is right and when some of the Vassilissis Sofias houses were built *in the late nineteenth century, they did indeed enjoy a river view. Now, as well as ruined temples, Athens has ruined rivers. Her water, like so many other mysteries and myths of the city, lies buried underground. The famous brooks and springs of antiquity – the Klepsydra Spring which nurtured a budding civilization – are all gone. And the River Ilissus whose prospect must have enhanced the view of the rich and the pleasure of ordinary citizens existed most famously as it tumbled at the foot of Mount Arditou, where this last walk wanders.*

The eighteenth and early nineteenth-century Grand Tourists, who painted Athens as a place of sublime desolation, did show a stream running just outside the city walls. But their Athens is little more than a large and sudden rock with some decaying accretions, set in a desert of hazy ochres and purples. What stands out clearly in this forgotten landscape is the columns of the **Temple of Olympian Zeus** and the **Arch of Hadrian**; in their solitude they are instantly recognizable to anyone familiar with the city today.

The Arch of Hadrian is a good place to start an exploration of this area. It is ten minutes' walk from the Akropolis metro and stands, slightly isolated, to the far side of hectic Vassilissis Amalias, though perhaps the best view of it is from the far end of Lyssikratous to the north-west. From there, in foreshortened view, it looks very much like the city gate it once was.

Two inscriptions on the arch of Hadrian set out his vision for the city. On the north-western (Acropolis) side it says: *This is Athens, city of Theseus* (its legendary founder). And on the other side: *This is the city of Hadrian and not of Theseus.*

In pursuit of his grand plans for the city, and for his own immortality in architecture, Hadrian built a whole new quarter for Athens, much of which has disappeared under the aggregation of the centuries. But remains from this period are continually being revealed, sometimes by deliberate archaeological excavation, sometimes almost accidentally in the course of building works: some in the adjacent tropical lushness of the Zappion Gardens, others in Adrianou and around the Roman *agora*.

> The fifteen majestic columns now alone remaining of the mighty temple of Jupiter Olympus, are usually abandoned to a solitude and stillness so intense, that there seems to hang around them a very atmosphere of desolation. Which singularly enhances the awful sublimity of these ancient ruins.
>
> Christopher Wordsworth, writing in 1832–3

Just beyond the Arch is Hadrian's greatest bequest. It too was an unequivocal message about Roman power and it remains so. The Temple of Olympian Zeus, the largest temple in Greece, had stood unfinished for 700 years when Hadrian decided to complete and dedicate it in 130 CE, the year of his last and most triumphant visit to Athens. Tradition had it that one of the chasms around which myths and water eddied as ancient floods disappeared underground was once on this spot. A much earlier temple – long vanished even by Hadrian's time – had been erected, and the floods and the gods constrained and placated with offerings of flour and honey, thrown through strange fissures in the earth.

Fifteen tremendous marble columns of Hadrian's building survive and are still dizzyingly impressive. Originally there were 104. When Hadrian dedicated the temple it contained an immense statue of Zeus and (with a degree of self-regard that is astonishing to us but would not have been to the subjects of Imperial Rome) a companion statue of Hadrian himself. Grateful – or pragmatic – Greek provinces sent further statues, until the great courtyards were full of Hadrian's images, a sort of hall of mirrors in marble. Twenty-one columns survived until the fifteenth century: one was rendered down for lime to build a mosque during the Turkish occupation, and another fell victim to Euros' winter violence, as did the west façade of the Erechtheion on the Acropolis, in the great storm of October 1852. The statues are scattered to the winds of time.

The entrance to the site is off Vassilissis Olgas. Immediately beside the entrance a small undistinguished path leads off into one of the most significant pieces of countryside of early Athens. If (as can happen) the access is closed, turning right at the next main road (into Arditou – an extension of Vassilissis Konstantinou) will bring you alongside a well-maintained athletics club and Olympic swimming pool. From the corner of its car park (or indeed at any stage between, along this stretch of road and where it turns right again onto Diakou) there are numerous unofficial but well-used paths down into a small valley.

Here, between three busy roads, is the dried-up river bed of the ancient **River Ilissus**, which rose on **Mount Hymettus**. It may tremble with classical associations but it also has all the simple charm of a garden. The Ilissus disappeared under tarmac and concrete from 1939 onwards but at the end of the fertile pocket of trees, rocks and wild flowers the dark bridge that supports the main roads roaring above the old watercourse has a sooty mouth as forbidding and impenetrable as any mythical abyss.

●

SOCRATES: It is indeed a lovely spot for a rest. The plane is very tall and spreading, and the *Agnus castus* splendidly high and shady, in full bloom too, filling the neighbourhood with the finest possible fragrance.

And the spring which runs under the plane; how
beautifully cool its water is to the feet. The figures
and other offerings show that this place is sacred to
Achelous and some of the nymphs. See too how
wonderfully delicate and sweet the air is, throbbing
in response to the shrill chorus of the cicadas – the
very voice of summer.

Plato: *Phaedrus*

The geography and botany of this part of the river is
pleasingly, if airily, congruent with Plato's descriptions. They
are also absolutely recognizable in the charming and
workmanlike drawings of the eighteenth-century emissaries of
the Society of Dilettanti, Revett and Stuart. The waters seem
to have vanished just moments before one arrives on the scene.
Here are the miniature gorges through which the river must
have fragmented and tumbled before opening out into the
broader, calmer bed that precedes the bridge. Here are the wild
flowers – hollyhock, acanthus and mullein – the aromatic
herbs and the overhanging fig, chestnut, olive and plane trees.

It is a place for contemplation (one old man sits alone in the
shade of a boulder reading his paper) and for ardent but careful
lovers, whose discarded condom wrappers in the most tangled
thickets are small but effective advertisements for Athens's
most successful drugstore: *The Hondos Centre*. Plato's *agnus
castus* or chaste berry, a plant that flourishes in the damp
environs of riversides, still grows here, its haze of purple flowers
moving with the bees. It has been famed since antiquity as a
remedy for excessive sexual desire. And the cicadas still sing.

. . . In a deep and shaded valley near the monastery,
whose banks are shaded with the *Agnus castus*,

oleaster and willow, we found the stream of the Ilissus
and a great number of Albanian women on its banks
employed in washing linen – picturesque enough in
the mass but possessing very few individual charms.
The sides of the Ilissus are marked by the foundations
of buildings which in former times encroached upon
its transparent stream, when the spreading plane trees
on its bank afforded a delicious retreat for the
voluptuary or the philosopher.

Thomas Smart Hughes, 1813

Emerging again onto the roadside, the church of **Ag. Fotini** is
half-hidden under the trees. The church exists in pleasing
conjunction with a probable rock-cut shrine to Pan. His
outline can be discerned by those predisposed to see it, his
haunches squatting on the wall at right angles to the church.

Crossing Arditou, to the foot of Mount Arditou, steep streets
to the left cross yet another of Athens's quiet former suburbs
which is slowly returning to fashionable status. Restoration of
1930s houses and the upgrading of once-simple tavernas have
not greatly altered the quiet decency of the area known as
Mets, which took its name from the German-owned brewery
Metz, founded here in 1870. The brewery was itself named
after a famous battle of the Franco-Prussian War; its owner was
a Herr Fuchs who, in pursuit of modernity, changed *his* name
to Fix and his beer followed suit. Herr Fix's building, on
Kalirois, is another clever industrial conversion, now housing
the exuberant **National Museum of Contemporary Art**.

This is a walk through ascending residential streets, with
plenty of shady oleanders and lemon trees, handrails on
steeper sections and the occasional restaurant. In many ways
it is harder to imagine Mets in its opportunistic nineteenth-
century heyday, noisy with music halls, cafés, small theatres

and some particularly popular brothels (*pantremenadika*), while windmills on the ridge even exploited the hillside breezes, than to envisage it as the ancient and solemn place of law and religion that it once was.

The most straightforward walk – or preferably stroll – is to turn left at the Arditou Kalirois intersection, up Anapafseos (Eternal Rest Street). Halfway up, at number 20, is a remarkable small museum and gallery (open Wednesday and Saturday by prior arrangement. Tel: 9232568). This is the house and studio of a woman painter and sculptor, **Loukia Georganti**, and the museum houses her own works and those of her parents in the place where they were created. Georganti is well known in Greece for her public sculptures and the gallery contains some of these life-size likenesses, plus small replica monuments such as the theatre of Herodes Atticus as it was in 1936; fantasies, including a mermaid; landscapes and sketches of traditional costumes. The heart of these displays is the gallery of china statuettes of the individuals whom she

Neoclassical wrought ironwork

immortalized full-scale elsewhere. Here, as though in a miniature Madame Tussaud's, are politicians, royalty and celebrities, all only thirty centimetres high.

After a steep climb, Anapafseos delivers the weary walker to the top of the hill and a more enduring nineteenth-century foundation than Herr Fix's brewery: the magnificent **Proto Nekrotafio Athinon**, the First Cemetery of Athens, laid out in 1837.

Poignant, grandiose, intriguing and only at times melancholy, this is a resting place (not necessarily the last; some incumbents only pass through, their remains being moved after three years) for the well-connected. It is both a museum of social history, an art gallery and a dense and exotic park. It is also a busy place where crowds of chatting mourners in deep black constantly pass to and from the chapels to the gravesides, eating *koliva* – the ritual cake of sunflower seeds, wheat, pomegranates, almonds and parsley – and burning incense for the deceased. To explore both the ancient Keramikos – diagonally opposite, on the far side of the city – and the modern Proto Nekrotafio is to conclude that the sorrows, rituals and celebrations of death have not changed much in two millennia.

Today only those who go to join their ancestors in a family vault or who (like the late Prime Minister Andreas Papandreou or the actress and politician Melina Mercouri) receive state funerals, are admitted to this most elite of cemeteries. In the past not only notable Greeks and one and a half centuries' worth of haut-bourgeois Athenians but also Philhellenes of many nationalities were interred along its crowded avenues. Here Heinrich Schliemann rests almost as impressively as he did in the palace of Troy – his mansion on Panepistimiou – in an immaculate classical mausoleum carved with reliefs of his Trojan exploits, while Adolf

Furtwängler awaits the Resurrection under a marble sphinx. Byron's friend, the historian and independence warrior Sir George Finlay, lies beside his wife and young daughter in the separate Protestant section.

Between the cypresses and the pines and the tropical shrubs there is one tomb marked with a single, two-metre-tall marble book, some winsome angels looking more like flower fairies, a striding Man of the People in sportswear and line upon line of whiskered and upright generals, with accompanying corseted matrons embroidering into eternity. A touching and life-size scene depicts two children, the little boy in a sailor suit, clustering around their father's deathbed. Do they mourn their lost years as well as their young parent as they stand in front of him, seventy years later? Here are the brave leaders of the Greek Wars of Independence, the poet and Nobel Prize-winner George Seferis, and the philanthropist Benakis all lying tidily under tall trees. Here are bishops clustered in preferential plots around the mortuary church. Statuary gives way to the all-too-compelling photograph – a politician is pictured smoking the pipe carved on his gravestone – as the twentieth century rolls on its way. In the list of names and long lives on one venerable family plot is a nineteen-year-old son, shot, it states without further comment, by the Germans in 1944.

●

> I've been smoking steadily all morning
> if I stop the roses will embrace me
> they'll choke me with thorns and fallen petals
> they grow crookedly, each with the same rose
> colour
> they gaze, expecting to see someone go by; no
> one goes by.

George Seferis (1900–1971)

●

The most famous sculpture is probably the 1878 memorial to Sofia Afendaki, known as **The Sleeping Maiden**, by Yannoulis Khalepis. In execution it is flawless; in spirit it has all the morbid sentimentality of a Victorian novel. In the stiff folds of the maiden's skirt, admirers frequently deposit a limp red rose of the sort that diners at Athenian restaurants are importuned to buy for wives and girlfriends.

Not far away is a much more terrible reminder of the reality of death. Near the entrance gate to the cemetery is a bronze memorial to the 40,000 Athenian victims of the German occupation and famine of 1941–3, carved by Costas Valsamis. A cadaverous, starved woman, her head thrown back, a baby hopeless at her breast, lies, appropriately, on barren earth.

Outside the cemetery gates old ladies, more fortunate in years than many of those within, sell votive candles and the small specialist shops that flourish in the shadow of death offer the elaborate beribboned floral arrangements, mounted on tripods, by which respect for the deceased's family is measured. In pole position, opposite the gates, is a splendidly imposing mortuary cake-shop, *Mnemosyne*, founded in 1938. Inside, serious bakers in immaculate whites stand behind cool counters, creating their ephemeral sculptures, while a young man with an undertaker's gravity presides over the order book. In the window are the ornate and pristine examples of their trade, sparkling in the Athenian light, their icing as pure as Pentelic marble. Exquisitely curled and plaited borders with crystalline flowers enclose the names of the dead – Maria, Dimitris, Elena – picked out in silver sugar balls.

Leaving the cemetery, bear right across the wide street and follow Trivonianou, which becomes Klitomahou. Turn left at Arhimidous and left again into Agras along the undulations of the Arditou Hill. This crosses a slightly old-fashioned residential area known as Stadiou which overlooks the wooded hillside as it follows the contours of the **Olympic Stadium**.

Known locally as Kallimarmaro Stadium, this open arena lies in a natural valley to the east of the Arditou hill. The main entrance is on Vassilissis Konstantinou (continuing along the main road, forking into Vassilissis Olgas, brings you back to The Temple of Olympian Zeus). From any approach the stadium is a highly distinctive monument, curved cleanly and brightly into the hillside.

From the air what you are likely to take in first is the great valley filled with off-white apartment buildings. All seemingly the same design and height. Stretching from the sea at the edge of the airport to what appear to be haze-shrouded mountains outlining a bowl-shaped horizon. You can find a certain definition in the few open spaces – sometimes green, sometimes brown, sometimes bald – that interrupt the spread of concrete to offer now and then a thing suddenly remarkable: a high white hill with a shaved crown like a monk's tonsure capped by a whitewashed church with a flag on a pole beside it for the cap's feather, the hill called Lycabettus; or a smaller hill, the more familiar Acropolis, with temples under scaffolding and not one but two open-air theatres of weathered marble; and just beyond the green oasis that used to be the Royal Garden, a narrow horseshoe of a stadium in the ancient style, restored at the turn of the century in pure white marble to serve the first of the modern Olympic games.

Edmund Keeley: *Inventing Paradise*, 1999

JEUX OLYMPIQUES A ATHÈNES
Notre compatriote Masson, vainqueur de la course vélocipédique

The first stadium was probably erected here in the fourth century BCE but for the Panthenaic games of 144 CE the wealthy philanthropist and self-aggrandizer Herodes Atticus reseated it in Pentelic marble. His tomb (inaccessible) is probably on the eastern side of this fine memorial.

In the ensuing centuries, mirroring the fortunes of the city, the stadium fell into disuse and disrepair and its stones were reused elsewhere. By Ottoman times it was a well-known haunt of witches. The stadium was rebuilt in 1896 as the centrepiece of the modern Olympic Games, a year which also saw the first marathon race follow the gruelling last journey of the hoplite Pheidippides, who ran from the battlefield of

Marathon to the city in 490 BCE to announce the Athenian victory against the Persians, before expiring of exhaustion. To massive excitement Greece took her only gold medal in the 1896 games when the race was won not by a trained athlete but by a local man, Spiros Louis. This still has a powerful hold on the Athenian imagination; local joggers who run just outside the perimeter of the stadium, inspired by its energetic associations, have now been given their own floodlit track.

In the summer of 2003, just over a year before the Olympics were due to return to Athens, the papers were full of dire warnings of heatwave death. The city had become a sluggish, dusty oven. Dogs lay immobile in the streets. The Athenians revived only at dusk; during the day, the streets of Plaka and the great archaeological sites were the preserve of the tourists in their specially bought travelling clothes.

Yet the idiosyncratic Greek justice system stirred itself to charge two immigrant building workers who had found the energy allegedly to dishonour the Greek flag that had been flying on the building site, which they were said to have pulled down and burned. To burn anything extra in such murderous heat would seem, regardless of symbolism, both brave and imbecilic.

Meanwhile, a nervous outside world was waiting to see if the city would be ready to meet the challenges and reap the rewards of the Games that they had been fighting to host for a decade. The view of the comfortable West, which still regards Greece as something Balkan and capricious, was sceptical, the papers swift to report that there were serious delays on all the building projects, that Athenians were encouraging prostitutes to prepare for an influx of clients. Would the infrastructure be in place? Would security be adequate? Would they do something about the pavements? Would they learn to be nicer to animals? In short, did the Greeks understand their Olympic responsibilities?

The Athenians of that summer, even those indifferent or hostile to the Games, had few anxieties about the deadline, though they were not immune to irritation at the persistent, excitedly apprehensive foreign criticism; they know the way things are done in their country. They had also seen a city transformed over the preceding five years. They had put up with the perpetual building works, the closures, the grit, the inconvenience and the cost, and had seen the slow emergence of fine archaeological parks, broad pedestrian streets, a superb new airport, an efficient Metro.

Tickets were selling at last, and volunteers – in a culture that does not have a tradition of voluntary service – had come forward in far greater numbers than expected; Greeks from the diaspora were returning home and those evading national service were being given a temporary amnesty if they returned to volunteer.

The stadium and its crane may have been boarded from public observation while the restoration work was completed, but a view-hole was left and what could be seen appeared close to perfection. You could see the workmen, right on the perimeter; tiny figures against the huge and graceful curve of marble, yet again repairing the furthermost tiers of the stone seating. The track was clean, the ranks of flagpoles white and ready. A year later, in August 2004, the Italian, Stefano Baldini entered the stadium to the applause of the crowd. It was a race not without incident; the man in lead place, Vanderlei de Lima, was pushed off the track by a protestor, but he gracefully accepted the bronze medal in the true spirit of the games. By contrast, two of Greece's own top athletes, several doctors and some police officers were involved in a scandal that was as visible as it was unfortunate, but the Olympics as a whole were a triumph; they were well-organized, safe, and a tastefully contrived reminder of Greece's great heritage. Some Athenians questioned whether the long-term benefits had been worth the estimated cost and disruption but, for a while, it was a time when Athens' history and its hopes for the future came together and Greece could rightly demand the world's respect.

As in daytime there is no star warmer and brighter than the sun, likewise there is no competition greater than the Olympic Games.

Pindar, fifth century BCE

RESTAURANTS, CAFÉS, SHOPPING AND HOTELS

Athens's numerous restaurants get better and better. The choice below is a tiny selection from some excellent possibilities. The slow introduction of elements of cooking from other countries has enriched the Greek menu and an interest in authentic traditional cooking has meant that the best of Greek food is worth seeking out. While nothing like the bargain that it was a decade ago, food is still good value in Athens. Greek wine has made enormous advances and wine from the Peloponnese or Crete now competes with more established European varieties, although it is only just beginning to appear in wine merchants outside Greece.

RESTAURANTS

At the top of the range, restaurants like **Spondi** (Michelin 1 *) Pironos 5, **Pangrati**, **Boschetto**, Evangelismo Park, **Pil-poul**, Apostolou Pavlou, **Thissio** or **Symbosio** (below) are as good as any in Europe. But it is in two culinary areas that Athenian restaurants succeed particularly well. One is with seafood, which comes fresh from the central market. It is not cheap but it is usually extremely good. The other is the traditional, unostentatious taverna, doing what it has done best for decades: grills, salads and baked dishes.

Stars indicate more expensive establishments, + ones that are special within their own class.

+***Symbosio**, Erehthiou 46, **Makrigiani**. Lovely house and courtyard and convenient for dinner after performances at the Theatre of Herodes Atticus. Specializes in game.

*_Daphne's_, Lyssikratous. On the edge of **Plaka**. Sophisticated versions of Greek food in fine neoclassical house.

Strofi, Rovertou Galli 25, **Makrigiani**. Traditional taverna a few minutes from the Acropolis in ordinary-looking house with wonderful views from its upper floor and friendly family-run service.

*_Mamacas_, Persefonis 41, **Gazi**. Slightly self-consciously fashionable restaurant with excellent and innovative take on Greek food – cooked by the owners' mothers.

Athenaikon, Themistokleous 2, **Omonia**. _Mezhedes_. Very traditional interior and service little changed since it opened in 1932.

+*_Vythos_, Ag. Asomaton 9, on corner with Adrianou, **Thissio**. Impeccable service, dining on the street. Fish at its best. Wine list comprehensive (but in Greek).

+_Kouklis_, Tripodon 14, **Plaka**. Delightful traditional taverna, very friendly. Wide choice of _mezhedes_ brought to you on a tray. Peaceful spot in one of Plaka's least-spoiled streets. A first choice for lunch.

Xinou, Angelou Geronda 4, **Plaka**. Old-fashioned garden dining in restaurant of character, with a largely Athenian clientele.

+_O Glikis_, Angelou Geronda 2, **Plaka**. Lunch deep under the vines at the end of a quiet residential street. Traditional choices, good puddings. Very laid-back. Table wine is simple and good.

+_Café Avyssinia_, Plateia Monastiraki. At the heart of the **Monastiraki flea market**, with unusual and delicious Macedonian specialities in a folk-meets-Art Nouveau interior. Music and crowds at weekends.

Diporto, Socrates 9, **Omonia/Food Markets**. Fish, lamb, chickpeas, cold retsina. Basic and good. Under an olive shop.

O Platanos, Diogenous 4, **Plaka**. In quiet square under the eponymous plane tree. Remains charming despite being popular with locals and visitors.

Diogenes, Plateia Lysiscrates. Expensive but comfortable and delightfully situated café right by **Monument of Lysiscrates** by day. Smartish outdoor restaurant by night.

+***Tou Psarra***, Erehthiou 16, **Anafiotika**. Seafood is especially good here and the situation, tucked away in the prettiest of back streets, is perfect. Ask to sit by the little church of St John the Theologian, not on the noisier terrace.

Taverna tou Psirri, Aeschylou 12, **Psirri**. Naxos-inspired dishes. Very good fish and cheese.

+***O Damigos***, Kidathineon 41 (under Vrettos distillery), **Plaka**. Founded in 1885 and still serving cod in various manifestations, as well as retsina. The authentic, old-fashioned Plaka experience but closed between late May and September.

* O Kafenion, Loukianou 26. Below the Lycabettus funicular, a quieter and upmarket **Kolonaki** restaurant with excellent *mezhedes*.

To Steki tou Ilia, Thessalonikis 7, **Thissio**. Lamb chops rule but salads and other grills available. Very popular with Athenians – get there early.

*Cellier Le Bistrot, Panepistimiou 10 (arcade). Just off **Syntagma**. Delicious main meals or lighter snacks in large, cool space. High quality wines by the glass.

+***Yiantes***, Valetsiou 58, **Exarchia**. *Yiantes* are the spicy butter beans that are one of the robust pleasures of Greek food. Organic produce is served in a pretty garden.

Something different: ***Arkhaion Yevesis***, Kodhratou 22. **Nr. Omonia**. Re-creation of the cuisine (though not the prices) of Ancient Greece, draped slaves, earthenware goblet and all. But no *hetairae* (serving girls).

CAFÉS

+***O Tristato***, Angelou Geronda, corner with Daedalou, **Plaka**. Puddings, cakes, tisanes, coffee and a fifty-year time warp.

Loumbardiaris, Filopappou, Ag. Dimitrios Loumbardiaris. A blissful and peaceful spot on the hillside, under the trees, within minutes of the Acropolis. Right by the church of the same name.

Kotsalis, Adrianou 112, **Plaka**. The Kotsalis family have run this peaceful and immaculate 'dairy-pastry' shop since 1906. Heavenly cakes, milk shakes, and tea.

55, Kalidromiou 55, **Exarchia**. Typical relaxed young café, convenient for Saturday-morning market.

Ydria, Adrianou, **Aerides**. Soft sofas and wicker chairs in tree-filled shady *plateia* by Hadrian's Library.

O Kipos, Irodou Atikou 4. A peaceful hideaway inside the **National Gardens**, with clambering greenery, a grotto and little iron tables.

Bee, corner Miaouli/Themidos, **Psirri**. Fashionable, young and charming café-bar with music.

SHOPPING

Aristokratikon. Kar. Servias 9, just off **Syntagma**, is a tiny chocolatier. From chocolate-dipped fruits or rose petals to jars of preserved quince or baby apples, all beautifully packaged, this is a delicious shop to see and smell and sample.

Cellier, Kriezotou 1, **Syntagma**. Learn and buy from this wine and liqueur merchant, expert in Greek varieties (also owns *Cellier Le Bistrot*, above).

Rentzis, Ipokratous 13. Stoa Operas. When in Athens ... Possibly the oldest tobacconist's in the city, with a vast range and an enthusiast's breadth of knowledge about cigarettes and cigars.

Mesogaia, Nikis 52, **Plaka**. Home-made foods, organic produce, cheese and delicious savoury foods – marinated anchovies, capers and preserves.

Tzegos. Fish and specialist cheese, butter, vegetables and bread from the produce-rich island of Naxos.

HOTELS

Hotels in Athens still do not offer the variety that most other European capitals take for granted. While there are several luxury hotels in Athens, most of these are modern and somewhat bland. The best hotels are largely outside Athens itself.

In the city small but comfortable hotels of character are thin on the ground. Many of the larger neoclassical houses would make wonderful town hotels but this has yet to happen.

Prices vary according to demand and are likely to soar in August 2004 when the Olympics are on.

LUXURY

The Grande Bretagne. [210 333 0000] Built in the mid-nineteenth century, in a league and a price bracket of its own. **Syntagma Square**. www.hotelgrandebretagneath.gr

St George Lycabettus. [210 729 0711] Kleomenous 2. www.sglycabettus.gr Immaculate hotel in a wonderful situation in a leafy street on edge of Kolonaki, and at the foot of **Lycabettus**.

Divani Palace Acropolis. Luxury hotel, within minutes of the **Acropolis**. Everything you would expect of a hotel in this category plus a length of original defensive walls of Themistocles on view in the lobby.

FAIRLY EXPENSIVE

The Herodian, Rovertou Galli 4, **Makrigiani**. Modern and newly refurbished but in a quiet and attractive street minutes away from **Plaka** and the Acropolis.

Andromeda, Timoleontas Vassou 22. Smallish boutique hotel in quiet surroundings. Sleek modern interior, strangely blending Italian and Polynesian style. A little out of the way but convenient for museums and **Kolonaki** shopping.

Electra Palace, Nicodimou 18. Elegant modern hotel but with a swimming pool complete with view of the Acropolis and perfect for **Plaka**.

INTERMEDIATE

The Cecil, Athinas 39. A colourful, sometimes noisy, but interesting area near the **markets**. A recently restored old building, with a friendly welcome but no public sitting areas.

Adrian, Adrianou 74. Heart of **Plaka**. Terrace, views of Erechtheion. Clean and convenient and simple comforts.

Achilleas, Lekka 21, between shops of **Ermou** and cultural centre of Panepistimiou. Simple, comfortable rooms, recently refurbished. Inner courtyard with abundant greenery.

Athenian Inn, Haritos 22. Pleasant accommodation, no luxuries but has open fireplace and is near to Lycabettus, in quiet street of small shops in **Kolonaki**. Lawrence Durrell stayed here on his many trips to Athens.

BUDGET

Art Gallery, Erehthiou 5, **Makrigiani**. As its name suggests, a house owned by an artist in which his paintings are displayed. It also has a little library of guidebooks and other nice touches in an otherwise very simple hotel.

Acropolis House, Kodrou 3, **Plaka**. Slightly eccentric, faded neoclassical pension down quiet street in **Plaka**. View of the Acropolis is from the corridors. Old murals and pleasant atmosphere but rather shabby, though spotless, bedrooms.

Phaedra. Simple. Shared showers but lovely position opposite Ag. Ekaterini, **Plaka**, and a minute from Plateia Lysiscrates.

FURTHER READING

For over two and a half thousand years, Athens has inspired writers of every kind, so any selection of books on the city and its culture must inevitably be arbitrary. The following short list of books by both Athenians and foreign visitors comprises commentaries, histories, plays, novels and poetry. All have been selected simply for their special ability to reflect the drama of Athens's past and the complexities of its present.

ANTIQUITY

Aristophanes, *Four Plays*
Thucydides, *History of the Peloponnesian War*
Plutarch, *The Rise and Fall of Athens*
James Davidson, *Courtesans and Fishcakes* (HarperCollins 1997)
Debra Hamel, *Trying Neaira: the True Story of a Courtesan's Scandalous life in Ancient Greece* (Yale University Press 2003)

GRAND TOURISTS AND REVOLUTIONARIES

David Brewer, *The Flame of Freedom: the Greek War of Independence 1821–1833* (John Murray 2001)
George Gissing, *Sleeping Fires* (1895)
John L. Tomkinson, *Traveller's Greece: Memories of an Enchanted Land* (Anagnosis 2002)

THE ASIA MINOR CATASTROPHE

Michael Llewellyn Smith, *Ionian Vision: Greece in Asia Minor, 1919–1922* (C. Hurst and Co. 1998)

WAR

Mark Mazower, *Inside Hitler's Greece* (Yale University Press 1995)

Henry Miller, *The Colossus of Maroussi* (1941)

Petros Haris, *The Longest Night: Chronicle of a Dead City* (Nostos 1985)

THE 1970S AND THE DICTATORSHIP OF THE COLONELS

Maro Douka, *Fool's Gold* (Kedros 1991)

MODERN GREECE

James Pettifer, *The Greeks: the Land and People since the War* (Viking Books 1993)

Patricia Storace, *Dining with Persephone* (Granta 1998)

Diane Shughart, *Athens by Neighbourhood* (Ellinka Grammata 2001)

Nick Papandreou, *Dancing with my Father* (Kedros 1996)

Cavafy, Sikelianos, Seferis, Elytis and Gatsos, *Voices of Modern Greece: Selected Poems* (Princeton University Press 1981)

ARCHITECTURE

Athens: from the Classical Period to the Present Day (C5 BCE–2000 CE) (Oak Knoll Press 2003)

City Guide: Athens (Blue Guides 2002)

Erica Protestou, *Athens: a guide to recent architecture* (Ellipsis 1998)

HISTORIES OF HISTORY

Mary Beard, *The Parthenon* (Profile Books 2002)
William St Clair, *Lord Elgin and the Marbles* (Oxford
Paperbacks 1998)

ENVOI

And when I should remember the paragons of
    Hellas
I think instead
Of the crooks, the adventurers, the opportunists,
The careless athletes and the fancy boys,
The hair-splitters, the pedants, the hard-boiled
    sceptics
And the agora and the noise
Of the demagogues and the quacks; and the
    women pouring
Libations over graves
And the trimmers at Delphi and the dummies at
    Sparta and lastly
I think of the slaves.
And how one can imagine oneself among them
I do not know;
It was all so unimaginably different
And all so long ago.

Louis MacNeice, *Autumn Journal IX* (1939)

INDEX

Numbers in italics refer to illustrations.

About, Edmond, 100–1, 146
Academy of Athens, 123
Academy, Panepistimiou, *134*
Achille, Georgiou, 110
Achilleas (hotel), 186
Achilles (road), 83
Acropolis
  approaches to, 36
  clearing of houses, xiii
  by day and night, 4–5, 41
  entrance, 41
  maps, *33*
  in midsummer, xxviii
  Museum, 42–3
Acropolis House (hotel), 186
Adrian (hotel), 186
Adrianou, 11–12, 16, 17, 22–4,
    55, 56, 57, 61, 62–3, 64,
    167, 184, 186
Aerides, xxv, 25, 80
Aeschylou, 106, 183
Aeschylus, 38, 64
Aeschylus (street), 104
Afendaki, Sofia, 174
Ag. Assomati, 55, 76, 81
Ag. Athanassios, 66
Ag. Dimitrios, 102–4
Ag. Dimitrios Loumbardiaris,
    46, *46*, 184

Ag. Dinami, 77
Ag. Ekaterini, 7, 186
Ag. Eleftherios, 77–8
Ag. Filipos, 62
Ag. Filotheis, 78
Ag. Fotini, 170
Ag. Georgios, 139
Ag. Georgios tou Vrachou (St
    George of the Rock), 8
Ag. Ioanis stin Kolona, 105
Ag. Ioanis Theologos, 15
Ag. Irini, 100
Ag. Nikolaou Rangavas, 15
agnus castus, 169–70
Agora, xiii, 29, 57–9
  see also Roman Agora
Agras, 174
Aigli (restaurant), 147–8
Akademias, 120, *134*, 135
akrokerama (terracotta carv-
    ings), 75, 110
Akropolis metro station, 35, *37*
Alexandreia (restaurant), 133
Amalia, Queen, 145–6
American School of
    Archaeology, 58
American School of Classical
    Studies, 138
Anafiotika, 8–9, *8*, 11

Anapafseos, 171, 172
Andromeda (bookshop), 125
Andromeda (hotel), 185–6
Andronicus Kyrrhestes, xxiii
Androutsos, Odysseas, 9, 10
Angelou Geronda, 18–19, 182,
    183
antiparohi system, xvi
antique shops, 111, 113
Apeliotes (east wind), xxiv
Aphrodite of Knidos (statue), 65
Apostolou Pavlou, 44, 50, 57,
    64, 68, 181
Apotheke (theatre), 107
Arch of Hadrian, 55, 146, 166–7
Archaeological Book Service,
    125
Arditou, 168, 170
Arditou Hill, 175
Areopagus, 43, 44, 64
Areos, 24, 30
Arhimidous, 174
Aristides, 48
Aristokratikon (chocolate
    shop), 184
Aristophanes, 38
Arkhaion Yevesis (restaurant),
    183
Armenian Church of Athens,
    105
Arsakeio Building, 126
art galleries
    Epistrofi, 108
    Frissiras Museum of
        Contemporary Art, 18
    National Museum of
        Contemporary Arts,
        Mets, xv, 170
    Psirri, 107–8
    Vergina gallery, 51
Art Gallery (hotel), 186
Art Theatre, 126–7
Artemidos, 108
Asclepion, 38–9
Asia Minor Catastrophe, xx, 26
Aspasia, 106
Asty (cinema), 124–5
Athena, 75, 123, 139
Athena Polias, 42
Athenaeum, 62–3
Athenaeus, 98–9
Athenaikon (restaurant), 129,
    182
Athenäis, Metaxourgeio, xv
Athenian Inn (hotel), 186
Athens
    ancient, xiv–xv
    architecture, xvi–xvii, 44–5,
        119–20
    as birthplace of democracy, 48
    Byzantine, 9, 77, 81, 119
    as capital city, xiii
    charm of, xxii
    culture, xv–xvi
    immigrants, 93
    Ottoman, xiii, 22, 26, 27–8,
        77, 93, 95
    place names, xxxi
    renovation, xviii
    Roman, 10, 22, 25, 26, 29, 39,
        55, 57, 149, 157, 166–8
    and the seasons, xxvii–xxx
    smog, 140–1
    water, 165–6
Athens Festival
    (June–September), 39, 125

Athens–Piraeus Electric
    Railway (ISAP), 68
Athens School of Fine Arts, 64
Athens Stock Exchange, 104,
    126, 128
Athinas, 79, 80, 97, 99, 102, 186
atomiko poikilia, 56
Attalos (restaurant), 56
Auerbach, Frank, 18
autumn, xxix

Bairaktaris (restaurant), 95–6
Bairaktaris, D., 105
Balbilla, Julia, 47
Barber, Robin, xxxi
Bathhouse of the Winds, 27–8
Bee (music bar), 106, 184
Benaki Museum, 133, 153
Beulé Gate, 41
Blue Guide to Athens, xxxi
bookshops, 110, 125–6, *126*,
    131, 158
Boreas (north wind), xxiv, 75
Boschetto (restaurant), 181
Boulanger (architect), 120
boxing hall, Ermou, 81, *82*
Brewer, David, 10
British Council, 136
British School of Archaeology,
    138
brothels, 171
Byron, George Gordon, Lord
    and Greece, xiii, 3–4
    love affairs, 106–7
    memorabilia, 138
    monument to, 4, *5*
    quoted, 3
Byzantine Museum, 151, *152*

Caesar, Julius and Augustus, 26
Café Avyssinia, 108, 109, 182
Café Kalidromiou, 130
cafés, *55*, 183–4
    The Five Brothers, 29
    I Eftihia Sto Gazi, 89
    Kotsalis, 23, 184
    Loumbardiaris, 184
    Milos, 130
    O Kipos, 149, 184
    O Tristato, 19, 183
    Ydria, 24, 184
    Zonar's Café, 44
    see also restaurants; tavernas
Callas, Maria, 63
Cambas, Andreas, 62
Capodistrias, Count John, 123
cappuccino freddo, 63
Caravan (patisserie), 135
Casson, Lionel, ix
Cave of the Furies, 65
The Cecil (hotel), 186
Cellier (wine shop), 184
Cellier le Bistrot (restaurant),
    122–3, 183
cemeteries
    Keramikos, 76, 81, 85–6, 172
    Proto Nekrotafio Athinon,
        122, 172–4
chair shops, *108*
Chandler, Richard, 25–6
Charlemont, Lord, 49
child entertainers, 93–4
Childe Harold's Pilgrimage
    (Byron), 3–4
Chinatown, 128
chocolate shops, 184
Choniates, Michael, 78

Choregic Monuments, 13, 25
Chrysa, 137
Church, Sir Richard, xiii, xxxi
churches/chapels
  Ag. Assomati, 55, 76, 81
  Ag. Athanassios, 66
  Ag. Dimitrios, 102–4
  Ag. Dimitrios Loumbardiaris,
      46, 46, 184
  Ag. Dinami, 77
  Ag. Ekaterini, 7, 186
  Ag. Eleftherios, 77–8
  Ag. Filipos, 62
  Ag. Filotheis, 78
  Ag. Fotini, 170
  Ag. Georgios, 139
  Ag. Georgios tou Vrachou (St
      George of the Rock), 8
  Ag. Ioanis stin Kolona, 105
  Ag. Ioanis Theologos, 15
  Ag. Irini, 100
  Ag. Nikolaou Rangavas, 15
  Armenian Church of Athens,
      105
  English Church of St Paul,
      158
  Kapnikarea, 79
  Metamorfosis tou Sotera
      (Church of the
      Transfiguration of the
      Saviour), 9, 17
  Mikropolis (Old Cathedral),
      77–8
  Mitropolis (Cathedral), 77
  Panayia Gorgeopiköos, 77–8
  Panayia Hrissospiliotissa
      (Our Lady of the Golden
      Cave), 38
  Roman Catholic Cathedral of
      St Denis, 123
  Russian Church of Sotira
      Likodimou, 157–8
Churchill, Winston, 156
cigarettes, consumption, xix
cinemas
  Asty, 124–5
  Ciné Paris, 19, 20–1
  Lipton Ice, 107
  Thiseion, 64
City of Athens Cultural
    Centre, 134
City of Athens Museum, 120
Colonus, 83–4
Compendium (bookshop), 158
concert halls, xv
Connolly, Cyril, 41
Constantine, King, xx
costume shops, 23
Craven, Lady Elizabeth, 28
criminal courts, 105

Daedalus, 42
Damaskinos, Archbishop, 17
Daphne's (restaurant), 6–7, 182
Demetrios Rallis Mansion, 124
Demosthenes, 4, 64
Dexameni Square, 136
Dexipou, 24
Diakou, 168
Diogenes, 4
Diogenes (restaurant), 183
Diogenous, 28–9, 182
Dionissiou Areopagitou, 5–6,
    36–7, 44, 50
Dionysos, 38, 65
Dionysos Restaurant, 44, 50

Diporto (ouzeri), 101, 182
Dipylon Gate, 86
distilleries, 21
Divani Palace Acropolis
    (hotel), 185
dogs, 64
Douglas, F.S.N., 43
Douka, Maro, 132, 150

Eden (restaurant), 16
Eftimiadi, Neni, 139
Electra Palace (hotel), 186
Eleftherios Venizelou
    (Panepistimiou), xvi, 104,
    119–27, 157, 183
Eleftheroudakis (bookshop),
    126
Eleusis, 86
Elgin, Lord, 3
Elytis, Odysseas, 36, 139, 153
Enastron (taverna), 106
English Church of St Paul, 158
Eolou, 24, 29, 100
Epaminonda, 30
Epidavros, 39
Epistrofi (art gallery), 108
Epitafios, 141
Eptahalkou, 65
Erechtheion, 35, 41, 42, 43,
    123, 168
Erehthiou, 16, 40, 181, 183, 186
Eridanous River, 85
Ermou, 75, 76, 79, 80–1, 85,
    108, 157
Ethnikos Kipos, 146–7
Euripides, viii, 38
Euros (south-east wind), xxiv
Evangelismos, 137, 181

Evangelistrias, 78
Evripidou, 99–100, 99, 102,
    105
Evzones, 150, 154
Exarchia, 125, 129, 130

'The Fair Maid of Athens'
    (Byron), 106–7
fan shops, 80
fastfoodadika, xvi, 131
Festival of Dionysia, 38
Festival of Music, xxviii
Fethiye (Victory) Mosque, 26
Figoures and Koukles (shadow
    theatre), 13
Filelinon, 157, 158
Filopappou, 184
Finlay, Sir George, xiii, 173
First University of Athens, 11
The Five Brothers (café), 29
flea markets, 108–9, 111, 182
food markets, 97–8
food shops, 184, 185
Frissiras Museum of
    Contemporary Art, 18
fruit and vegetable market, 98
funicular railway, 137, 139
Furtwängler, Adolf, 172–3

galaktobouriko, 23
Galt, John, 7, 41
gardens, 145–51
Garston, Edgar, 155
Gate of Athena Archegetes, 26
Gatsos, Nikos, 84
Gazi, xvii, 55–6, 68, 85, 86–90
    gasometers, 86–7, 88
Gennadion Library, 138–9

Gennadiou, 138
Gennadius, John, 138
Georganti, Loukia, 171–2
George, King, 140
Geraniou, 128
gigantes, 15
Gissing, George, 56, 141
Gladstone, William Ewart, 123
Gonia tou Agroti, 133
Goulandris Museum of
    Cycladic and Ancient
    Greek Art, 152–3
Grande Bretagne (hotel), 119,
    155–6, 185
Great and Little Cathedrals
    (square), *112*, 113
Great Idea period, xx
Greece
  independence, xiii, xx, 3, 9,
      77, 104, 173
  Jewish community, 17–18
  Junta, xx, 131
Greek Orthodox Church, xxvi-
    ii, 7, 77
Greeks, character, xviii, xix–xx,
    xxi–xxii
Gregorious V, 123
Guru (music bar), 106

Hadrian, Emperor, 22, 26, 47,
    55, 166–8
Hadrian's Library, 24, 56
halva, 20
Hansen, Christian Frederik,
    120, 124
Haritos, 186
Harmony Square, 127
Harrison, James Albert, 82

Hellenic Cosmos, Tavros, xv,
    87–8
Hephaeston (Temple of
    Hephaestus), 10–11, 25, 55,
    56, 58, 59–60
Hermes, 75–6
Herodes Atticus, 176
The Herodian (hotel), 185
Hill of the Nymphs, 44, 50
Hill of the Muses, xxv, 44, 46
Horologion, xxiii–xxvi, 10, 25,
    26, 29
horta, 15
hotels, 185–6
Hughes, Thomas Smart, 169–70
Humphreys, William, 10

I Eftihia Sto Gazi (café), 89
Ieros Odos (Sacred Way), 86, 89
Ifestou, 56, 109, 110
Iliou Megathron (Palace of
    Troy), 120, *121*
Ilissus River, 151, 166, 168–9
Ipokratous, 125, 184
Iraklio, 133
Iraklidon, 64, 67, 68
Irodu Atikou, 149, 150, 151,
    184
Ivi (theatre), 107

Jewish community, 17–18
Jewish Museum, 17–18, 158
Justinian, Emperor, xiv

kafenion (restaurants), xxiii,
    xxix
Kaftanzoglou (architect), 120,
    121, 123, 126

Kaikas (north-east wind), xxiv
Kakourgiodokiou, 105
Kalirois, 170
Kalidromiou, 125, 130, 133, 184
Kallimarmaro Stadium, 175–7
Kanari, 135
Kanellopoulos Museum, 10
Kapnikarea, 79
Karaisaki, 108
Karytakis, Mr, 81
Kauffman (bookshop), 126
Keeley, Edmund, 175
Kentriki Agora, 97–8
Keramikos (cemetery), 76, 81, 85–6, 172
Khalepis, Yannoulis, 174
Kidathineon, 11–12, 17, 18–21, 183
Kiristou, 16, 27–8
Kleanthis (architect), 120, 126
Kleisthenes, 48
Kleomenous, 185
Klepsydra Spring, 166
Klitomahou, 174
Kodhratou, 183
Kodrou, 17, 186
koliva, 172
Kolonaki, 133, 135–6, 141, 151
Konstantinopolous, 83
Korai (plaza), 124
korai (statuettes), 43
Korais, Adamantios, 123
Korovezes, Mr, 61–2
Kotsalis (dairy café), 23, 184
Kouklis (taverna), 14, 182
Koumandareas, Menis, 94–5
Koumbari, 133, 154
koutsavakides, 105

Kriezi, 105
Kriezotou, 184

La Maison d'Antiquités, 50
laterna (barrel organ), 79, 96
Lear, Edward, 138
Lekka, 186
Lenormant, Charles, 83
Likavittos, 8
lions, stone, *xxiv*
Lips (south-west wind), xxiv
Lipton Ice (cinema), 107
Louis, Spiros, 177
Loukianou, 136, 137, 183
Loumbardiaris (café), 184
Lycabettus Hill, 104
Lysicrates, 4
Lyssikratous, 13, 166, 182

MacNeice, Louis, 191
Mahaffy, J.P., 40
Makri, Teresa, 106–7
Makrigiani, 50–1
Mamacas (restaurant), 88, 182
maps, x, xi, 2, 32, 33, 54, 72, 73, 92, 116, 117, 144, 164, 207
Marbois-Lebrun, Sophie de, Duchesse de Plaisance, 151–2
Mardonius, 42
Martinos (antique shop), 111, 113
Mavromihali, 125, 127
Mazower, Mark, 60, 150–1
Megaron Concert Hall, xv
Melanthiou, 102
Melina Mercouri Cultural Centre, 67–8

Melissinos, 110–11
Menandrou, 105, 128
Mercouri, Melina, 172
Merrill, James, 142
Mesogaia (food shop), 184
Metamorfosis tou Sotera
    (Church of the
    Transfiguration of the
    Saviour), 9, 17
Metaxas dictatorship, xx
metro system, 158–61, *207*
Metropolis (music shop), 127
Mets, xv, 170–2
mezhedes, 14, 19, 56
Mikon, 106
Mikonos, 106
Mikropolis (Old Cathedral), 77–8
Miller, Henry, 148
Milos (café), 130
Missolonghi, 3, 138
Mitropoleos, 77
Mitropolis (Cathedral), 77
Mitropoulos, Costas, xviii
Mnemosyne (cake shop), 174
Mnisskleous, 22, 28
Monastiraki, xxv, 55, 56, 69,
    93–104
Monastiraki flea market,
    108–9, *111*, 182
Monastiraki Square, 76
Moni Petraki, 138
Monis Asteriou, 18
Monument of Lysiscrates, 4,
    13, 25, 183
Mount Arditou, 166, 170
Mount Hymettus, 140, 168
Mount Lykavittos, xxv, 134,
    136–7, 139–41, 154

Mount Parnassus, xxx
Moraitis (artist), 23–4
Morosoni, Captain-General, 16
Moussio Polemiko (war muse-
    um), 152
Muller, Karl Ottfried, 83
Museum of Ceramics, 95
Museum of Greek Folk Arts, 18
Museum of Greek Folk Music,
    29
Museum of the Ancient Agora,
    59
Museum of Theatre, 135
museums, xxv
    Acropolis Museum, 42–3
    Benaki Museum, 133, 153
    Byzantine Museum, 151, *152*
    City of Athens Museum, 120
    Frissiras Museum of
        Contemporary Art, 18
    Goulandris Museum of
        Cycladic and Ancient
        Greek Art, 152–3
    Jewish Museum, 17–18, 158
    Kanellopoulos Museum, 10
    Loukia Georganti museum,
        171–2
    Moussio Polemiko, 152
    Museum of Ceramics, 95
    Museum of Greek Folk Arts,
        18
    Museum of Greek Folk
        Music, 29
    Museum of the Ancient
        Agora, 59
    Museum of Theatre, 135
    National Archaeological
        Museum, xxvi, 132–3

National Historical Museum, 120

National Museum of Contemporary Arts, Mets, xv

Numismatic Museum, 121

music, xxviii, 29, 63, 79, 96–7, 101–2, 106, 126–7

Muslim Medresse, 27, 27

Nafplion, 120

Nargis (restaurant), 128

National Archaeological Museum, xxvi, 132–3

National Gardens, xxix, 146–7, 147, 149, 165, 184

National Historical Museum, 120

National Library, 123, 124

National Museum of Contemporary Arts, Mets, xv, 170

National University, 123–4

Naxos (taverna), 106

Neapolis, 133–4

nefos (smog), 140–1

Neofytou Douka, 153

Nicodimou, 186

nightclubs, 89

Nikis, 17, 158, 184

Notos (south wind), xxiv

Numismatic Museum, 121

O Damigos (restaurant), 21, 183

O Glikis (café), 19, 182

O Kafenion (restaurant), 137, 183

O Kipos (café), 149, 184

O Platanos (restaurant), 29, 182

O Tristato (café), 19, 183

Oasis (restaurant), 146

Odos Ag. Assomaton, 81

Odos Thissio, 60

Oedipus, 83–4

Oktovriou, 132

Olympia Theatre, 134

Olympic Games, xvii, 159, 176–9

Olympic Stadium, 175–7

Omirou, 123

Omonia, 93, 119, 127–9, 133

Omonia Square, 165

Oresteia (Aeschylus), 38, 64

Orfeos, 88

Otto, King, 5, 25, 59, 77, 127, 145, 149, 154

Ottoman baths, 27–8

ouzeris, xxix, 101

Panagi Tsaldari, 67, 85, 86, 89

Panayia Gorgeopiköos, 77–8

Panayia Hrissospiliotissa (Our Lady of the Golden Cave), 38

Pandora (musical instrument shop), 127

Pandrossou, 109–11, 113

Panepistimiou (Eleftherios Venizelou), xvi, 104, 119–27, 157

arcade, 125–6, 183

Panos, 10, 29

Pantheon (Roman), 22

pantremenadika (brothels), 171

Papandreou, Andreas, 172

Papandreou, Nick, viii
Parthenon, *xiv*
  admission to (1835), xiii
  as arsenal, 25
  fame of, 35–6
  image of, xiii–xiv, 40–1
  marbles, 3, 5, 35
  patisseries, 135
Patriarhi Ioakim, 136
Pausanias, 24
Pelopida, 29
Pericles, 48, 106
  funeral oration, 86
periptero (kiosks), xviii, *xix*, 51, 66
Persefonis, 88, 182
Pesmazoglou, 126
Phaedra (hotel), 186
pharmacies, 158
Pheidippides, 176–7, 178
Pheraios, Constantine, 123
Philhellenes, xiii
Philip of Macedon, 25
Philopappus, 44, 47
Philopappus, Julius, 47
Phryne, 64–5
Pikilis, 30
Pikionis, Dimitris, 45, 46, 161
Pil-Poul hat factory, 67–8, 83
Pindar, 178
Piraeus, 165
Pironos, 181
Plaka, xxv
  and Byron, 3–4
  cafés, 18
  centre, 11–12
  character, 4–5
  graffiti, *xxi*, 5, 30

  houses, *xxix*, 13–14, 16
  restaurants, 12, 14, 15, 16, 29
  street corners, *11*
  tourist information, *12*
Plapouta, 133
Plateia Avissinias, 60, 80, 108
Plateia Exarchion, 130
Plateia Filikis Etairias, 136
Plateia Filomoussou Etairias, 11–12, 18, 55
Plateia Iroon (Square of the Heroes), 104, 105
Plateia Kolonakiou, 135, 154
Plateia Lysiscrates, 4, 6, 7, 183
Plateia Mitropoleos, 77, 78
Plateia Monastiraki, 30, 80, 93, 95, 182
Plateia Omonia, 152
Plato, 45–6, 168–9
Plato's Academy, 82, 83, 84–5
Platonos, 83
Ploutarhou, 139
Pnyx, xxviii, 44, 46, 48–9, *48*
poikilia, 19
Polignotou, 30
Polytechnic University of Athens, xx, 131
Poulopoulou, Elias, 67
Praxiteles, 64
Proto Nekrotafio Athinon (cemetery), 122, 172–4
Protopsalti, Alkestis, 109
Psipsina (taverna), 106
Psirri, 80, 105–8

rebetika clubs, xxx, 101–2
Rebetika Istoria, 101
Rego, Paula, 18

religious festivals, xxviii
Rentzis (tobacconist), 184
restaurants
   Aigli, 147–8
   Alexandreia, 133
   Arkhaion Yevesis, 183
   Athenaikon, 129, 182
   Attalos, 56
   Bairaktaris, 95–6
   Boschetto, 181
   Café Avyssinia, 108, 109, 182
   Cellier le Bistrot, 122–3, 183
   Daphne's, 6–7, 182
   Diogenes, 183
   Dionysos, 44, 50
   Eden, 16
   kafenion, xxiii, xxix
   Mamacas, 88, 182
   Nargis, 128
   O Damigos, 21, 183
   O Glikis, 19, 182
   O Kafenion, 137, 183
   O Platanos, 29, 182
   Oasis, 146
   Spondi, 181
   Symbosio, 40, 181–2
   Ta Tria Gourounakia, 136
   To Steki tou Ilia, 66–7, 183
   To Treno sto Rouf, 90
   Tou Psarra, 15–16, 183
   Vythos, 63–4, 182
   Yiantes, 183
   see also cafés; tavernas
Rizari, 152
Roman Agora, 10, 25, 26, 29, 55, 57, 167
Roman baths, 149, 157
Roman Catholic Cathedral of

St Denis, 123
The Rossikon, 127
Rouf, 86
Rouf Station, 89
Rovertou Galli, 40, 44, 50, 51, 182, 185
Royal Gardens, 145–6
Russian Church of Sotira Likodimou, 157–8

Sacred Gate, 86
Sacred Way (Ieros Odos), 86, 89
St George Lycabettus (hotel), 185
St Paul, 43, 65
Santer, Jacques, xvii
Saronic Gulf, 140
Schedia (theatre group), 89
Schliemann, Heinrich, 120–1, 139, 172
Schubert (architect), 120
Seferis, George, 18, 42, 48, 139, 153, 154, 173
Servias, 184
Sina, 123
Sisyphus (taverna), 16
Skiron (north-west wind), xxiv
Skoufa, 136
'The Sleeping Maiden' (sculpture), 174
Socrates, 25
Socrates (street), 182
Sofokleous, 126, 128
Solonos, 125
son et lumière, xxviii, 48
Sophocles, 38, 83–4
Sophocles (street), 104
Souanatos, Dimitris, 22

Souidias, 138
Spondi (restaurant), 181
spring, xxviii
Spyromiliou Gallery, 125
Stadiou, 120, 124, 125, 174
Stavropoulos, Costas, 51
Stoa Athenaton, 101
Stoa Bibliou (Arcade of Books),
    126, *126*
Stoa of Attalos, 58–9
Stoa Orfeos, 126
Stournari, 131
Strathatos Mansion, 153
Stratonos, 8
Street of the Evzones, 104
Strefi Park, 130
Streit, 100
Strofi (taverna), 40, 182
Sulla, 66
summer, xxviii
Symbosio (restaurant), 40,
    181–2
Syntagma, 17, 119, 133, 184
Syntagma ('Constitution')
    Square, 44, 76, 154, 156–7,
    158, 165, 185

Ta Tria Gourounakia (restau-
    rant), 136
Taverna tou Psirri, 106, 183
tavernas
    Kouklis, 14, 182
    Naxos, 106
    Psipsina, 106
    Sisyphus, 16
    Strofi, 40, 182
    Taverna tou Psirri, 106, 183
    Xinou, 19–20, 182

see also cafés; restaurants
Tavros, xv, 87
Technopolis, xv, 87, 89
Temple of Athena Nike, 9, 41
Temple of Hephaestus
    (Hephaeston), 10–11, 25,
    55, 56, 58, 59–60
Temple of Olympian Zeus, 166,
    167–8, 175
terrorist groups, xx, 131–2
Tessera (nightclub), 89
theatre
    Apotheke, 107
    Art Theatre, 126–7
    Ivi, 107
    Museum of Theatre, 135
    Olympia Theatre, 124
    Schedia, 89
    Theatre Exarchia, 129–30
    Thesion, 107
Theatre of Dionysos, 13, 37–8
Theatre of Herodes Atticus,
    xxviii, 37, 39–40, 171
Theatrou, 101
Thekla, 106
Themistocles, 48
Themistokleous, 129, 130, 182
Thermopilon, 83
Thesion, 55, 56, 58
Thesion (theatre), 107
Thespidos, 7–8, 13
Thespis, 38
Thessalonikis, 65–6, 67, 183
Thiseion (cinema), 64
Thissio, 44, 50, 55, 60, 62, 67,
    68, 76, 85, 90
Thrasillou street, 37
Thucydides, xx–xxi, 86

Timoleontas Vassou, 185
To Steki tou Ilia (restaurant),
     66–7, 183
To Treno sto Rouf (restaurant),
     90
tobacconists, 184
Tomb of the Unknown Soldier,
     154
Tou Psarra (restaurant), 15–16,
     183
Tower of the Winds, xxiii–xxvi,
     10, 25, 26, 29
Tripodon, 13, 14, 15, 182
Tripoleos, 83
Trivonianou, 174
Tsitsanis, V., 102
Twain, Mark, 65
Tzegos (food shop), 185
Tzina (music shop), 127
Tzisdarakis mosque, 95, 96

Valetsiou, 183
Valsamis, Costas, 174
Vassilissis Konstantinou, 168,
     175
Vassilissis Korovezes, 61
Vassilissis Amalias, 3, 166
Vassilissis Olgas, 3, 146, 168,
     175
Vassilissis Sofias, xv, xxv, 22,
     133, 138, 141, 151–3, 154,
     157, 165–6
Vergina gallery, 51
Vikelas, Yiannis, 153
Villa Ilisia, 151, *152*

Viosol, 87
Vironos (Byron), 6
Voukourestiou, 135
Vouli (royal palace), 154
Voulis, 77
Voutadon, 89
Vrettos (distillery), 21, 183
Vythos (restaurant), 63–4, 182

war museum, 152
winds, eight personifications of
     the, xxiv
wine shops, 6, 158, *159*, 184
winter, xxix–xxx
Wordsworth, Christopher, 58,
     167

Xenoglosso Vivliopoleio (book-
     shop), 125
Xinou (taverna), 19–20, 182

Ydria (café), 24, 184
Yiantes (restaurant), 183
yiayia, 18
Yofyllis, Fotos, 157

Zaharof, Vassilis, 137
Zappion, 147–51, 167
Zephyros (west wind), xxiv
Ziller, Ernest, 83, 120, 121–2,
     126, 153
Zogolopoulos, Giorgos, 160
Zonar's Café, 44
zoo, 149
Zosimus, 124

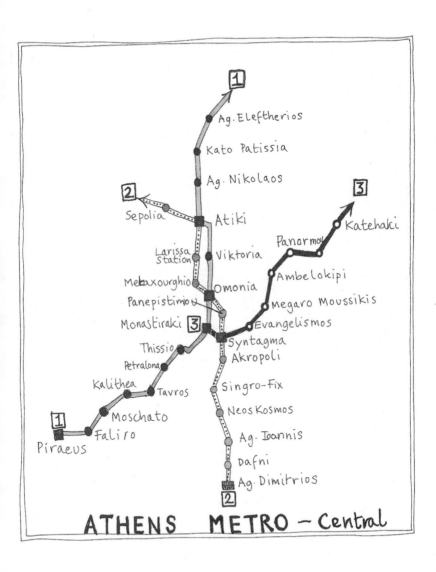

ATHENS METRO — Central